Gentleman Jack

The Official Biography of **Jack Sears**

Graham Gauld : Foreword by Sir John Whitmore

VELOCE PUBLISHING
THE PUBLISHER OF FINE AUTOMOTIVE BOOKS

Other great books from Veloce –

SpeedPro Series
4-Cylinder Engine – How to Blueprint & Build a Short Block for High Performance (Hammill)
Alfa Romeo DOHC High-Performance Manual (Kartalamakis)
Alfa Romeo V6 Engine High-Perf Manual (Kartalamakis)
BMC 998cc A-Series Engine – How to Power Tune (Hammill)
1275cc A-Series High-Performance Manual (Hammill)
Camshafts – How to Choose & Time them for Maximum Power (Hammill)
Cylinder Heads – How to Build, Modify & Power Tune Updated & Revised Edition (Burgess & Gollan)
Distributor-type Ignition Systems – How to Build & Power Tune (Hammill)
Fast Road Car – How to Plan and Build Revised & Updated Colour New Edition (Stapleton)
Ford SOHC 'Pinto' & Sierra Cosworth DOHC Engines – How to Power Tune Updated & Enlarged Edition (Hammill)
Ford V8 – How to Power Tune Small Block Engines (Hammill)
Harley-Davidson Evolution Engines – How to Build & Power Tune (Hammill)
Holley Carburetors – How to Build & Power Tune Revised & Updated Edition (Hammill)
Jaguar XK Engines – How to Power Tune Revised & Updated Colour Edition (Hammill)
MG Midget & Austin-Healey Sprite – How to Power Tune Updated & Revised Edition (Stapleton)
MGB 4-Cylinder Engine – How to Power Tune (Burgess)
MGB V8 Power – How to Give Your, Third Colour Edition (Williams)
MGB, MGC & MGB V8 – How to Improve (Williams)
Mini Engines – How to Power Tune on a Small Budget Colour Edition (Hammill)
Motorcycle-engined Racing Car – How to Build (Pashley)
Motorsport – Getting Started (Collins)
Motorsports Datalogging (Templeman)
Nitrous Oxide High-Performance Manual (Langfield)
Rover V8 Engines – How to Power Tune (Hammill)
Sportscar/Kitcar Suspension & Brakes – How to Build & Modify Enlarged & Updated 2nd Edition (Hammill)
SU Carburettor High-Performance Manual (Hammill)
Supercar, How to Build (Thompson)
Suzuki 4x4 – How to Modify for Serious Off-Road Action (Richardson)
Tiger Avon Sportscar – How to Build Your Own Updated & Revised 2nd Edition (Dudley)
TR2, 3 & TR4 – How to Improve (Williams)
TR5, 250 & TR6 – How to Improve (Williams)
TR7 & TR8, How to Improve (Williams)
V8 Engine – How to Build a Short Block for High Performance (Hammill)
Volkswagen Beetle Suspension, Brakes & Chassis – How to Modify for High Performance (Hale)
Volkswagen Bus Suspension, Brakes & Chassis – How to Modify for High Performance (Hale)
Weber DCOE, & Dellorto DHLA Carburetors – How to Build & Power Tune 3rd Edition (Hammill)

Those were the days ... Series
Alpine Trials & Rallies 1910-1973 (Pfundner)
Austerity Motoring (Bobbitt)
Brighton National Speed Trials (Gardiner)
British Police Cars (Walker)
British Woodies (Peck)
Crystal Palace by (Collins)
Dune Buggy Phenomenon (Hale)
Dune Buggy Phenomenon Volume 2 (Hale)
MG's Abingdon Factory (Moylan)
Motor Racing at Brands Hatch in the Seventies (Parker)
Motor Racing at Goodwood in the Sixties (Gardiner)
Motor Racing at Oulton Park in the 1960s (McFadyen)
Motor Racing at Oulton Park in the 1970s (McFadyen)
Short Oval Racing in the 1980s (Neil)
Three Wheelers (Bobbitt)

Enthusiast's Restoration Manual Series
Citroën 2CV, How to Restore (Porter)
Classic Car Bodywork, How to Restore (Thaddeus)
Classic Car Electrics (Thaddeus)
Classic Cars, How to Paint (Thaddeus)
Reliant Regal, How to Restore (Payne)
Triumph TR2/3/3A, How to Restore (Williams)
Triumph TR4/4A, How to Restore (Williams)
Triumph TR5/250 & 6, How to Restore (Williams)
Triumph TR7/8, How to Restore (Williams)
Volkswagen Beetle, How to Restore (Tyler)
VW Bay Window Bus (Paxton)
Yamaha FS1-E, How to Restore (Watts)

Essential Buyer's Guide Series
Alfa GT (Booker)
Alfa Romeo Spider Giulia (Booker & Talbott)
BMW GS (Henshaw)
BSA Bantam (Henshaw)
BSA Twins (Henshaw)
Citroën 2CV (Paxton)
Citroën ID & DS (Heilig)
Fiat 500 & 600 (Bobbitt)
Jaguar E-type 3.8 & 4.2-litre (Crespin)
Jaguar E-type V12 5.3-litre (Crespin)
Jaguar/Daimler XJ6, XJ12 & Sovereign (Crespin)
Jaguar XJ-S (Crespin)
MGB & MGB GT (Williams)
Mercedes-Benz 280SL-560SL Roadsters (Bass)
Mercedes-Benz 'Pagoda' 230SL, 250SL & 280SL Roadsters & Coupés (Bass)
Morris Minor (Newell)
Porsche 928 (Hemmings)
Rolls-Royce Silver Shadow & Bentley T-Series (Bobbitt)
Subaru Impreza (Hobbs)
Triumph Bonneville (Henshaw)
Triumph TR6 (Williams)
VW Beetle (Cservenka & Copping)
VW Bus (Cservenka & Copping)

Auto-Graphics Series
Fiat-based Abarths (Sparrow)
Jaguar MkI & II Saloons (Sparrow)
Lambretta LI series scooters (Sparrow)

Rally Giants Series
Audi Quattro (Robson)
Big Healey – 100-Six & 3000 (Robson)
Ford Escort MkI (Robson)
Ford Escort RS1800 (Robson)
Lancia Stratos (Robson)
Peugeot 205 T16 (Robson)
Subaru Impreza (Robson)

General
1½-litre GP Racing 1961-1965 (Whitelock)
AC Two-litre Saloons & Buckland Sportscars (Archibald)
According to Carter (Skelton)
Alfa Romeo Giulia Coupé GT & GTA (Tipler)
Alfa Romeo Montreal – The Essential Companion (Taylor)
Alfa Tipo 33 (McDonough & Collins)
Anatomy of the Works Minis (Moylan)
Armstrong-Siddeley (Smith)
Autodrome (Collins & Ireland)
Automotive A-Z, Lane's Dictionary of Automotive Terms (Lane)
Automotive Mascots (Kay & Springate)
Bahamas Speed Weeks, The (O'Neil)
Bentley Continental, Corniche and Azure (Bennett)
Bentley MkVI, Rolls-Royce Silver Wraith, Dawn & Cloud/Bentley R & S-series (Nutland)
BMC Competitions Department Secrets (Turner, Chambers Browning)
BMW 5-Series (Cranswick)
BMW Z-Cars (Taylor)
British 250cc Racing Motorcycles by Chris Pereira
British Cars, The Complete Catalogue of, 1895-1975 (Culshaw & Horrobin)
BRM – a mechanic's tale (Salmon)
BRM V16 (Ludvigsen)
BSA Bantam Bible (Henshaw)
Bugatti Type 40 (Price)
Bugatti 46/50 Updated Edition (Price & Arbey)
Bugatti T44 & T49 (Price & Arbey)
Bugatti 57 2nd Edition (Price)
Caravans, The Illustrated History 1919-1959 (Jenkinson)
Caravans, The Illustrated History from 1960 (Jenkinson)
Carrera Panamericana (Tipler)
Chrysler 300 – America's Most Powerful Car 2nd Edition (Ackerson)
Chrysler PT Cruiser (Ackerson)
Citroën DS (Bobbitt)
Cliff Allison - From the Fells to Ferrari (Gauld)
Cobra – The Real Thing! (Legate)
Cortina – Ford's Bestseller (Robson)
Coventry Climax Racing Engines (Hammill)
Daimler V8 SP250 New Edition (Long)
Datsun Fairlady Roadster to 280ZX – The Z-car Story (Long)
Dino – The V6 Ferrari (Long)
Dodge Charger – Enduring Thunder (Ackerson)
Dodge Dynamite! (Grist)
Draw & Paint Cars – How to (Gardiner)
Drive on the Wild Side, A – 20 extreme driving adventures from around the world (Weaver)
Ducati 750 Bible, The (Falloon)
Ducati 860, 900 and Mille Bible, The (Falloon)
Dune Buggy, Building a – The Essential Manual (Shakespeare)
Dune Buggy Files (Hale)
Dune Buggy Handbook (Hale)
Edward Turner: the man behind the motorcycles (Clew)
Fiat & Abarth 124 Spider & Coupé (Tipler)
Fiat & Abarth 500 & 600 2nd edition (Bobbitt)
Fiats, Great Small (Ward)
Fine Art of the Motorcycle Engine, The (Peirce)
Ford F100/F150 Pick-up 1948-1996 (Ackerson)
Ford F150 1997-2005 (Ackerson)
Ford GT – Then, and Now (Streather)
Ford GT40 (Legate)
Ford in Miniature (Olson)
Ford Model Y (Roberts)
Ford Thunderbird from 1954, The Book of the (Long)
Forza Minardi! (Vigar)
Funky Mopeds (Skelton)
Gentleman Jack (Gauld)
GM in Miniature (Olson)
GT – The World's Best GT Cars 1953-73 (Dawson)
Hillclimbing & Sprinting – The essential manual (Short & Wilkinson)
Honda NSX (Long)
Jaguar, The Rise of (Price)
Jaguar XJ-S (Long)
Jeep CJ (Ackerson)
Jeep Wrangler (Ackerson)
Karmann-Ghia Coupé & Convertible (Bobbitt)
Lambretta Bible, The (Davies)
Lancia 037 (Collins)
Lancia Delta HF Integrale (Blaettel & Wagner)
Land Rover, The Half-Ton Military (Cook)
Laverda Twins & Triples Bible 1968-1986 (Falloon)
Lea-Francis Story, The (Price)
Lexus Story, The (Long)
little book of smart, the (Jackson)
Lola – The Illustrated History (1957-1977) (Starkey)
Lola – All the Sports Racing & Single-Seater Racing Cars 1978-1997 (Starkey)
Lola T70 – The Racing History & Individual Chassis Record 3rd Edition (Starkey)
Lotus 49 (Oliver)
MarketingMobiles, The Wonderful Wacky World of (Hale)
Mazda MX-5/Miata 1.6 Enthusiast's Workshop Manual (Grainger & Shoemark)
Mazda MX-5/Miata 1.8 Enthusiast's Workshop Manual (Grainger & Shoemark)
Mazda MX-5 Miata: the book of the world's favourite sportscar (Long)
Mazda MX-5 Miata Roadster (Long)
MGA (Price Williams)
MGB & MGB GT – Expert Guide (Auto-Doc Series) (Williams)
MGB Electrical Systems (Astley)
Micro Caravans (Jenkinson)
Micro Trucks (Mort)
Microcars at large! (Quellin)
Mini Cooper – The Real Thing! (Tipler)
Mitsubishi Lancer Evo, the road car & WRC story (Long)
Montlhéry, the story of the Paris autodrome (Boddy)
Morgan Maverick (Lawrence)
Morris Minor, 60 years on the road (Newell)
Moto Guzzi Sport & Le Mans Bible (Falloon)
Motor Movies – The Posters! (Veysey)
Motor Racing – Reflections of a Lost Era (Carter)
Motorcycle Road & Racing Chassis Designs (Noakes)
Motorhomes, The Illustrated History (Jenkinson)
Motorsport in colour, 1950s (Wainwright)
Nissan 300ZX & 350Z – The Z-Car Story (Long)
Pass the Theory and Practical Driving Tests (Gibson & Hoole)
Peking to Paris 2007 (Young)
Plastic Toy Cars of the 1950s & 1960s (Ralston)
Pontiac Firebird (Cranswick)
Porsche Boxster (Long)
Porsche 356 (2nd edition) (Long)
Porsche 911 Carrera – The Last of the Evolution (Corlett)
Porsche 911R, RS & RSR, 4th Edition (Starkey)
Porsche 911 – The Definitive History 1963-1971 (Long)
Porsche 911 – The Definitive History 1971-1977 (Long)
Porsche 911 – The Definitive History 1977-1987 (Long)
Porsche 911 – The Definitive History 1987-1997 (Long)
Porsche 911 – The Definitive History 1997-2004 (Long)
Porsche 911SC 'Super Carrera' – The Essential Companion (Streather)
Porsche 914 & 914-6: The Definitive History Of The Road & Competition Cars (Long)
Porsche 924 (Long)
Porsche 944 (Long)
Porsche 993 'King of Porsche' – The Essential Companion (Streather)
Porsche 996 'Supreme Porsche' – The Essential Companion (Streather)
Porsche Racing Cars – 1953 to 1975 (Long)
Porsche Racing Cars – 1976 on (Long)
Porsche – The Rally Story (Meredith)
Porsche: Three Generations of Genius (Meredith)
RAC Rally Action! (Gardiner)
Rallye Sport Fords: the inside story (Moreton)
Redman, Jim – 6 Times World Motorcycle Champion: The Autobiography (Redman)
Rolls-Royce Silver Shadow/Bentley T Series Corniche & Camargue Revised & Enlarged Edition (Bobbitt)
Rolls-Royce Silver Spirit, Silver Spur & Bentley Mulsanne 2nd Edition (Bobbitt)
RX-7 – Mazda's Rotary Engine Sportscar (updated & revised new edition) (Long)
Scooters & Microcars, The A-Z of popular (Dan)
Scooter Lifestyle (Grainger)
Singer Story: Cars, Commercial Vehicles, Bicycles & Motorcycles (Atkinson)
SM – Citroën's Maserati-engined Supercar (Long & Claverol)
Subaru Impreza: the road car and WRC story (Long)
Taxi! The Story of the 'London' Taxicab (Bobbitt)
Tinplate Toy Cars of the 1950s & 1960s from Japan (Ralston)
Toyota Celica & Supra, The book of Toyota's Sports Coupés (Long)
Toyota MR2 Coupés & Spyders (Long)
Triumph Motorcycles & the Meriden Factory (Hancox)
Triumph Speed Twin & Thunderbird Bible (Woolridge)
Triumph Tiger Cub Bible (Estall)
Triumph Trophy Bible (Woolridge)
Triumph TR6 (Kimberley)
Unraced (Collins)
Velocette Motorcycles – MSS to Thruxton Updated & Revised (Burris)
Virgil Exner – Visioneer: The official biography of Virgil M Exner designer extraordinaire (Grist)
Volkswagen Bus Book, The (Bobbitt)
Volkswagen Bus or Van to Camper, How to Convert (Porter)
Volkswagens of the World (Glen)
VW Beetle Cabriolet (Bobbitt)
VW Beetle – The Car of the 20th Century (Copping)
VW Bus – 40 years of Splitties, Bays & Wedges (Copping)
VW Bus Book, The (Bobbitt)
VW Golf: five generations of fun (Copping & Cservenka)
VW – The air-cooled era (Copping)
VW T5 Camper Conversion Manual (Porter)
VW Campers (Copping)
Works Minis, The Last (Purves & Brenchley)
Works Rally Mechanic (Moylan)

WWW.VELOCE.CO.UK

First published in February 2008 by Veloce Publishing Limited, 33 Trinity Street, Dorchester DT1 1TT, England. Fax 01305 268864/e-mail info@veloce.co.uk/web www.veloce.co.uk or www.velocebooks.com.
ISBN: 978-1-845841-51-5/UPC: 6-36847-04151-9

© Graham Gauld and Veloce Publishing 2008. All rights reserved. With the exception of quoting brief passages for the purpose of review, no part of this publication may be recorded, reproduced or transmitted by any means, including photocopying, without the written permission of Veloce Publishing Ltd. Throughout this book logos, model names and designations, etc, have been used for the purposes of identification, illustration and decoration. Such names are the property of the trademark holder as this is not an official publication.

Readers with ideas for automotive books, or books on other transport or related hobby subjects, are invited to write to the editorial director of Veloce Publishing at the above address.
British Library Cataloguing in Publication Data - A catalogue record for this book is available from the British Library. Typesetting, design and page make-up all by Veloce Publishing Ltd on Apple Mac.
Printed in India by Replika Press.

Contents

Acknowledgements 4
Foreword by Sir John Whitmore 5
1 The Sears dynasty 7
2 Jack starts racing 20
3 British Saloon Car Champion 36
4 Dabbling in Formula 2 & an
   introduction to Ferrari 49
5 The Cortina days 62
6 More Cobras & the Brands Hatch
   incident 78
7 The Shelby American Cobra Coupé
   programme 88
8 The London-Sydney Marathon 100
9 David Sears – entrepreneur 110

Appendix 1 Stanley Sears and
   his Collection 121
Appendix 2 Race and Rally statistics 148
Bibliography 156
Index 159

Acknowledgements

One of the great pleasures of working with Jack Sears on a book like this is that he is the possessor of the most accurate memory of any racing driver I have ever met, as well as being the most erudite. Sure, there are others who can string stories together, but Jack's command of the entire sequence of his life in racing is quite remarkable. From time to time I questioned in my own mind the odd fact that Jack dropped into the conversation but, on checking, I found it was usually perfectly accurate. Not only that, but he has kept a meticulous record of his racing career from the very first event to the last, and this record – reproduced in the appendices at the end of the book – is a fascinating insight to the sheer variety of cars Jack has raced during his life. Not many people start out with 1914 TT Sunbeams and graduate to Ferraris and Shelby American Cobra Coupés at Le Mans.

They called him Gentleman Jack and few other racing drivers have looked the part: the well-groomed hair and well-cut clothes; his sheer politeness to everyone, it all fits, although Jack admits there were times when he cast aside the 'Gentleman' bit! Here is a man who, on the surface, is supremely organised but with a turmoil that boils to the surface if his meticulous plans are disturbed: he talks of his fury at being hauled up before the stewards at Brands Hatch after a race where he was called in for a stop-go penalty, and then stormed out of the pits shaking his fist and hurling uncomplimentary epithets left, right and centre.

I have many people to thank for help in creating this book; the poor author usually manages to miss out someone but, in the plethora of throw-away lines, passing remarks and telephone calls, I would like to acknowledge the help of just some old friends.

First of all the fellow drivers who raced and rallied with and against Jack: John Coombs, Mike McKee, Tommy Sopwith, Sir Jackie Stewart, Australian saloon car legend Bob Jane, and Henry Taylor. I would particularly like to thank some of Jack's oldest motor racing friends, such as Peter Riley who competed in his first event at the same time as Jack, and who drove with him in the BMC team at Le Mans and Sebring; Alan Mann for his assistance in the period Jack Sears raced the Shelby American Cobra Coupés for him in 1965; Tommy Sopwith, whose words were taken from an interview I conducted with him over ten years ago, and Stuart Turner, international rally co-driver and competitions manager for Castrol and Ford, etc, who added his own humorous stories concerning Jack.

Nowadays, one is almost obliged to check out the Internet for confirmation of small details. This can be dangerous as there are a lot of 'history makers' out there who would like to change known facts and introduce all sorts of conspiracy theories to straightforward and natural events. However, special thanks must go to the many contributors to the Nostalgia Forum (Atlas F1 Bulletin Board) who added a word here and a fact there, including "Wolf", Tim Murray, Alan Cox, David Beard and Simon Taylor. Various friends around the world also contributed interesting facts, including Carlos Guerra in Portugal and Rob Young in Durban, South Africa.

Most importantly, I must thank Jack, his wife, Diana, and Jack's family Suzanne, Jennifer and David, who put up with this intruder that kept asking questions.

Finally, thanks to James Paterson who first broached the idea of this book two years ago at the BRDC Silverstone Classic.

Graham Gauld
Claviers, France

Foreword
by Sir John Whitmore

Jack was the gentleman that I should have been. He had the grace, whilst I had only the title. I often told him that he should have had it rather than I, but he wasn't buying. Although he began racing several years before I did, our careers took a parallel path for much of the way, which gave me the privilege of getting to know him really well. That he was an outstanding driver is obvious, and you will have had this reaffirmed by the time you have read this book. That he has remained a loyal friend to me for nearly fifty years is something that only I can tell.

I first met and raced against Jack at the *Daily Express* Silverstone International in May 1959. He was in a big Healey and I was in one of the very first Lotus Elites. Stirling Moss, Roy Salvadori and Jack were on the front row of the grid; I was on the second row alongside Colin Chapman in another Elite. As a newcomer I was introduced to these awesome heroes. By the time we had become team mates at BMC and then at Ford, I had regained my sense of perspective: Jack was human, after all. One of our first travels together was in 1962 for BMC in the Sebring 12 hour race. Jack, who is more English than the English, appealed to the natives in Florida, all except the one whose baseball cap he snatched and threw off the footbridge over the track because he was blocking our path. This would have gone nuclear had I not intervened to separate the warring factions.

As Jack was usually so much calmer and better organised than me, he had a somewhat paternalistic way of keeping me in order when my tricks and humour went over the top. However, with that Sebring incident ever in mind, I was always ready to defend him if necessary. Jack and I were both East Anglia-based farmers, but there was a big difference between us; he actually knew the back end of a cow from the front, and what sugar beet looked like, while I elected experts to do that for me. We also shot pheasants with beaters and all that, from time to time, too, but he was better at the etiquette bit, and probably the shooting as well.

We were both committee members of the BRDC and directors of Silverstone in the mid-sixties at the time when the grass seed crop and the pigs were more relevant to the accounts than the circuit racing. I even talked Jack into learning to fly in my yellow Beech Musketeer. We had a lot of fun in those days, both at our respective homes and abroad, where it was by no means beyond Jack to behave badly in ways inappropriate to recount here, though I will say that he always did so with best manners and often with flowers.

It was in 1963 that Jack and I signed up with Ford for the rest of our careers. That winter we drove a Wilment Galaxie, a Cobra and a Lotus Cortina in various races in South Africa. While there, Jack mistook my enthusiasm for talent and tried to teach me golf with no success at all; I quickly discovered that, for me, it was a game too slow. Thereafter, we both drove works Daytona Coupé Cobras and Lotus Cortinas in the USA and round Europe, and had the time of our lives as well as many successes, much of which is recorded so eloquently in this book.

One popular photograph from those days is of Jack and I in the two Works Lotus Cortinas drifting at identical angles around Copse Corner at Silverstone. In that race we managed to pull off one of the few dead heats in racing, but not without some finger-wagging from Colin Chapman who thought we were both going to go off. As it turned out only one of us was on the grass – me, of course – as we finally crossed the finishing line side-by-side. Jack and I even managed the near-impossible and took a Cortina down the bobsleigh run at Cortina D'Ampesso in Italy, during an unscheduled interlude whilst celebrating the many Lotus Cortina championship achievements all over Europe in 1964.

The outrageous side of Jack was never far beneath his polite and elegant surface, but it is for his enduring friendship that I remember him most. It is always a joy to meet with him, as we still do at Goodwood and other events. He is one of those people in whom I could always confide, and to whom I could turn to for advice or help. He would never fail to respond as a true gentleman would. I have never managed to live up to his standards, but we both plan to be around for a long time – and I'll get there, Jack!

The Sears Dynasty

To all intents and purposes this story begins in Northampton in the year 1870 when the original John – known as Jack – Sears was born. Little is known about the Sears family before this date, but it must be assumed that it was of modest means as Jack left school at the age of 14 and was apprenticed as a cobbler. He proved to be very bright and quickly learned how to repair shoes; once he had completed his apprenticeship he left and started out in business on his own.

In the mid-1880s there was considerable demand not only for cobblers to repair shoes, but for bespoke shoes and boots also, so it was no surprise when Sears began to handcraft his own quality shoes. In time, he married Caroline Wooding and his new wife helped him in his shop.

One day Jack decided to stand outside the shop and listen to what his customers had to say; he quickly came to appreciate that, although his boots and shoes were highly regarded, they were too expensive. This led to a change in approach to shoemaking to the production of less expensive shoes for the masses, in the same manner as Henry Ford approached the manufacture of cars. Jack was instantly successful and was forced to start a small factory which then became a big factory. It is interesting that the name of the company, and his shops, was True-Form, a brand name which, to this day, is synonymous with modestly priced quality shoes.

When they married, Jack and Caroline Sears lived in a modest terraced house but as the business grew and grew they moved to a semi-detached house. In the early 1900s, Jack was in a position to buy Collingtree Grange, an impressive country house in the village of Collingtree just south of Northampton, by which time Jack and Caroline

Founder of the Sears family fortune was John (Jack) Sears. (Jack Sears Archive)

7

The Sears family home at Collingtree Grange, bought by Jack's grandfather. The house has been demolished and is today replaced by a housing estate. (Jack Sears Archive)

had a daughter, Florence. In 1903 Stanley Edward Sears was born, followed by a second son, John, seven years later. Our story, however, now centres around Stanley Sears and his family.

In the space of just 19 years Jack Sears, founder of the Sears shoe business, went from a 14 year old apprentice to a major shoe manufacturer with a considerable fortune. He did drive but, by now, his wife had a car and a chauffeur. Young Stanley Sears was fascinated by the family cars and would take every opportunity to hang around the chauffeur and ride in the cars from the garage round to the big house. Sadly, however, he hardly knew his father because Jack Sears died in 1916 at the young age of 46, when Stanley was just 13 years old.

Caroline Sears was left with the three children, the youngest of whom, John, was just six. Caroline was also left the majority of the shares in John Sears and Company (True-Form Boot Company Ltd).

At that time the chairman of the board of directors was a Mr Panther and he, with the board, developed the company whilst Stanley Sears completed his schooling and, later, his university career at Cambridge.

A very good friend of the family, Arthur Dickens, became something of a guardian to young Stanley Sears and helped to guide him into the big, wide world of commerce that awaited him. Stanley was educated at Eastbourne College, was an excellent shot, and became a member of the shooting eight, which, in turn, his son, Jack Sears, would duplicate many years later.

Clearly, with constant development of mechanisation in the shoe industry an engineering background was deemed vital, and so on leaving Eastbourne Stanley Sears went to Cambridge to study engineering. One gets the impression that he thoroughly enjoyed his three years at Cambridge as he was always fascinated and interested in engineering due to his early introduction to cars. His ambition was to join Rolls-Royce Motors as he had been captivated by the history of Rolls-Royce, but his mother finally persuaded him that he should really go into the family shoe business as he was the eldest son.

Stanley joined John Sears and Company in 1926 as a member of the board and soon became absorbed in the company, spending a lot of time developing the business by visiting customers' shoe shops around the country, which also gave him an excuse to indulge his passion for driving.

The following year, 1927, was an important one, both for Stanley and the Sears family business. Earlier Stanley's mother had fallen ill and needed a nurse at home during her recuperation. The nurse was Lilian Dunning, whom Stanley fell madly in love with and married. Then, in December 1927, the Sears company expanded greatly with the acquisition of the Leicester-based shoe retail chain Freeman Hardy Willis, which had 551 retail stores around Britain.

Stanley and Lilian Sears had two sons, Jack and Eric. Jack became the racing driver best known for his exploits with Listers, Jaguars, Ferraris and Cobras, whilst Eric, though he competed in the occasional event, concentrated on being a farmer in Gloucestershire until his passion for flying overtook him, whereupon he sold his farm and became a commercial airline pilot.

For ten years Stanley was a director of John Sears and Company, but found he had lost some of his interest in shoes and wanted to be more involved in pure engineering, as well as becoming a farmer. This latter interest developed shortly after his father, founder of the company, died. The family home, Collingtree Grange, had a large farm attached to it and Stanley's interest in farming grew from there. In 1936 he moved his family to Bolney, just north of Brighton, and a farm which backed on to the A23, the London to Brighton road.

Not long after the family had settled in, Stanley Sears took the dogs for a walk one Sunday to where his land met the London to Brighton road. He had heard that there was a veteran car run that day and went along to have a look. When he saw those old cars coughing and spluttering their way to Brighton he was totally captivated and wanted to get immediately involved. He rushed back to the house, deposited the dogs, got into his car and dashed down to Brighton to chat to those taking part and find out all he could about owning and running a veteran car. He came back full of enthusiasm and, without a great deal of thought, bought the first car that came along, a two-cylinder Darracq. However, this turned out to be far too slow and was traded in the following year for a four-cylinder Clement Talbot fitted with shaft drive, as opposed to the chain drive Darracq. The car is still in the Sears family and is owned by Jack Sears' niece, Jackie, who, with her husband and children, is a regular on the London to Brighton run.

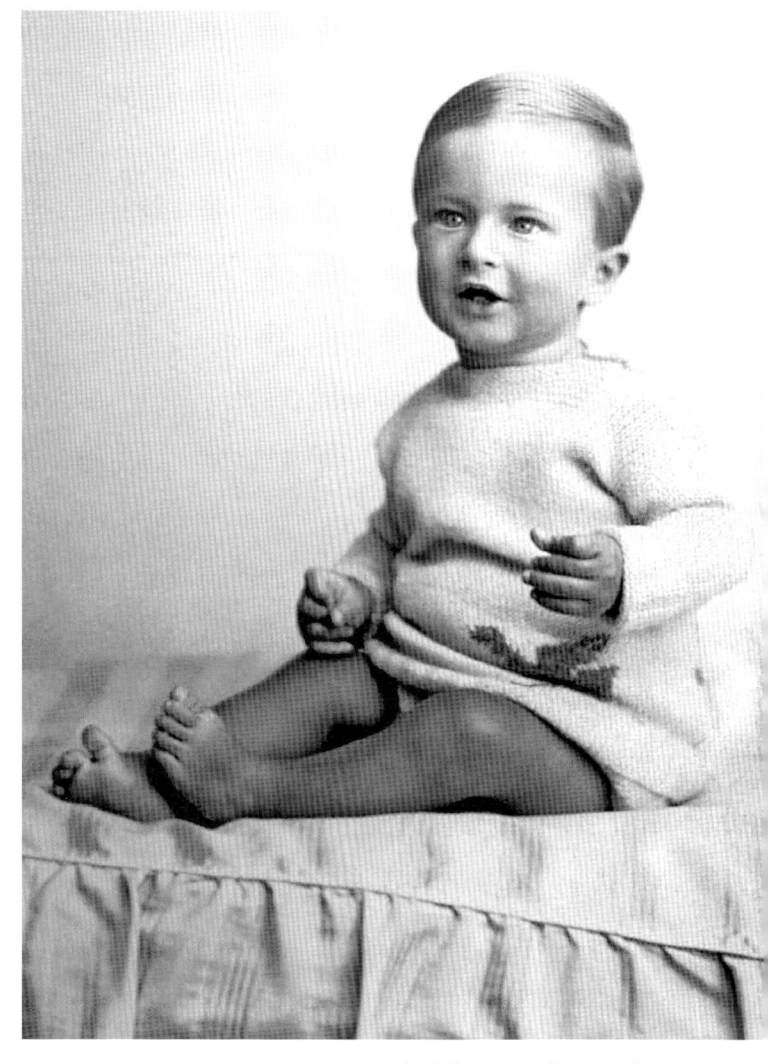

Jack Sears at the age of one.
(Jack Sears Archive)

Jack Sears was born in 1930. Though only six years old at the time Jack still remembers the move from Northampton to Bolney, having to pack up all his toys in boxes "... and saying goodbye to the big house and going to a new house. The house in Northampton was a town house down a cul-de-sac, and suddenly, the house we took over in Sussex, Bolney Place, was virtually in the middle of a village. I therefore, from the age of six, became interested in farming."

Jack Sears' early life was rather idyllic and his pride and joy was a child's car built by Vauxhall. He was six years of age when his parents bought him the Vauxhall pedal car which came complete with pneumatic tyres. Two years later his grandmother bought Jack and Eric another model car, this time powered and built by the Atco company, famous for its lawn mowers. Called the Atco Junior Safety-First Trainer, the model had a small motor mower engine at the back and a

Stanley Sears sits proudly at the wheel of his 1905 20hp Rolls-Royce with replica Tourist Trophy body. (Jack Sears Archive)

Jack and Cicely Sears at the wheel of the 1905 20hp Rolls-Royce, and Stanley Sears in the 1905 30hp Rolls-Royce. (Jack Sears Archive)

pull-up lever starter between the seats. Mechanically, it had one forward and one reverse gear, a clutch, a hand brake and an accelerator: a child's dream. The Atco was kept, maintained and, in turn, driven by Jack's son David and his sisters Suzanne and Jennifer. At the time of writing the Atco is being restored at David Sears' racing team headquarters for yet another generation of Sears.

The farm, Bolney Grange, was basically a chicken farming business specialising in 'petit poussin' (baby chickens) for the hotel trade. Stanley Sears and his partner, Mr Meekins, built the company into a large supplier of table-ready chickens. However, when war broke out Stanley Sears' partner died, leaving Stanley to run the farm throughout the war.

Another close neighbour was Peter Hampton who was a great collector of cars, particularly Bugattis, and a number of fine Bugattis passed through his hands. When war began, Hampton was enlisted in the Tank Corps and asked Stanley Sears to keep an eye on his cars and ensure the engines were turned over from time to time and kept dry.

Peter Hampton was badly wounded in the Allied landings on the Normandy beaches and lost the use of his left arm. He had always hoped an operation would restore some life to his arm but this never happened. As a result Hampton had the centre gear change on all his Bugattis transferred to the right-hand side. Jack Sears remembers an occasion when: "... he took me out in his supercharged Type 57 Bugatti soon after the war when I was about 18. I was absolutely amazed how competent he was as a driver with his one arm on the steering wheel and his other arm resting across his lap. As he couldn't move his left arm by itself it was quite remarkable how well he drove."

As a farmer Stanley Sears was not conscripted into the armed forces but was very active in the Home Guard, holding parades at Bolney Grange; an obvious meeting place as Stanley Sears was a keen rifle shot and had built his own rifle range on the farm.

Stanley had been an enthusiastic member – and later committee member and President – of the Veteran Car Club. Through the club he met up with Cullimore Allen, whose family company was John Allen and Sons (Oxford) which manufactured the famous Allen motorised scythes, a staple piece of equipment on any farm at the time; the company also made drainage machines. Through this close friendship, and Stanley's active interest as a farmer, Stanley was invited to become a director of John Allen and Sons, which was right up his street as it cast him back into engineering mode once more. As Stanley could speak French fluently (he had earlier been sent to France to learn the language), and John Allen and Sons was keen to establish itself in Europe,

THE SEARS DYNASTY

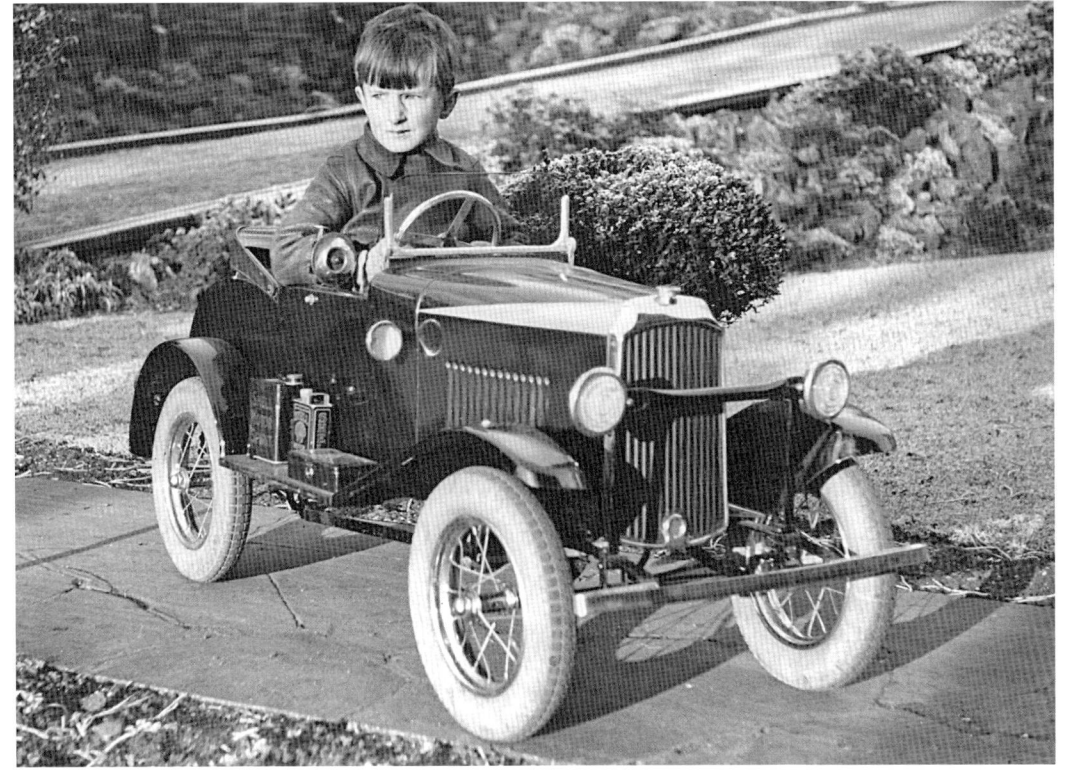

Jack and Cicely Sears at the wheel of the 1904 Mercedes on the London to Brighton run. (Jack Sears Archive)

First car: Jack Sears' first car was this replica Vauxhall 30/98 pedal car, given to him at the age of 8 by his father. (Jack Sears Archive)

GENTLEMAN JACK

The proud young Jack Sears poses in the brand new Atco Trainer bought for him by his grandmother. Today, the Trainer has been rebuilt for Jack's youngest grandson, Rory. (Jack Sears Archive)

Jack Sears' mother, Lilian Sears, proudly stands beside her Brighton concours-winning, 1927 Rolls-Royce Phantom 1. (Jack Sears Archive)

12

Sears was a regular competitor at the Brighton Speed Trials. This was his first ever Brighton sprint with his Morgan. (Jack Sears Archive)

he became the Export Director. The Frenchman chosen as the Allen concessionaire for France was Georges Staub, who became a regular visitor to the Sears household.

In 1944 at the age of 14 Jack was sent to one of England's best-known boarding schools, Charterhouse near Guildford. Here, he displayed many talents and, in particular, rifle shooting. Obviously, as a farmer's son his father had taught him to shoot from an early age, but at Charterhouse his enthusiasm for rifle shooting took him to a new level, and he was chosen to join the school shooting VIII that competed against other schools at the famous Bisley Ranges. His greatest success came at the age of 18, during his last year at Charterhouse, when the school won the Ashburton Shield, a competition that attracted teams from all the leading schools in the country.

By now the war had ended, and the teenage Jack Sears was growing up and driving around the farm in a cut-down Austin 16 converted into a flat bed truck with which to transport the chickens, which were free-range and so needed to be spread about. Whenever the Austin was not being used for transportation young Jack and his brother, Eric, practiced their driving skills on the farm roads in this and a 1914 FN two-seater. As this vehicle had a crash gearbox, the pair learned how to double declutch and change gear smoothly.

By the time he was 17, Jack had applied for a driving test and acquired his driving licence. As a birthday present his father gave him a sky-blue, 4+4 Morgan with a Standard ten engine. Said Jack: "It was my pride and joy and I just loved that little Morgan. My brother, Eric, was fourteen months younger than me and just over a year later when Eric passed his test, and unbeknownst to us, father sold the Morgan and bought us identical MG TCs. I had a cream one with red upholstery and Eric's was second-hand and red with red upholstery.

"I remember it well. One evening father told us he had

The Sears brothers' matching MG TCs at a local motor club event.
(Jack Sears Archive)

The sprint course at Bedwell Hey was an early training ground for Jack with his MG TC. (Jack Sears Archive)

something in the garage he wanted us to see. He slid the doors back and there were these two MGs sitting there: he said, 'That's yours and that's yours.' Can you imagine, we were over the moon!

"I had joined the Brighton and Hove Motor Club with my Morgan in 1948 and took part in driving tests and rallies, and even did the Brighton Speed Trials. I did the same with the MG in 1949."

At one of these events Jack met Peter Riley, a young man who was to figure prominently in his racing career much later. As Peter recalls: "My father had strictly forbidden me to race. The first time I put numbers on my car I had to use whitewash so that I could clean them off immediately afterwards. My first event was a Cambridge University speed trial at Bedwell Hey just outside Ely in Cambridgeshire. I entered my HRG 1500, and at scrutineering two cars behind me was this smart-looking fellow in an MG TC. We got talking and he told me it was his first time in competition. I said it was also mine and we got on famously. If someone had told us we would be sharing a car at Le Mans in ten years' time we would not have believed them."

Driving tests and speed trials were all very well but Jack Sears wanted more. "By 1950 I wanted to try a race. There was a BARC members meeting at Goodwood and I went down with no crash helmet, just a leather flying helmet. My father never thought about mentioning a crash helmet, and I had seen pictures of all the pre-war racing drivers without a helmet so it never occurred to me to wear a helmet. It was not a particularly successful race; I managed to spin the MG and then had to make up time. I think I finished fifth or sixth but it was a start."

Jack spent five years at Charterhouse public school and then began to think about his future. He could have embraced engineering, like his father, but his love of farming prevailed. On his father's advice, and with help from farming friends, Jack spent a year working on a farm. The following year, again to broaden his knowledge of farming, he spent six months working on a fen farm near Spalding, which meant he lived away from home in the Rose and Crown at Thorney. He then spent three months working for a specialist farm estate and land agent to give him an idea of farm valuations, and, finally, three months with a corn merchant that sold animal feeds. This two-year exercise demonstrated Stanley Sears' wisdom in giving Jack the opportunity to see farming from various standpoints, an experience which has moulded his farming career ever since. (It must be remembered that Jack Sears was never a fully professional racing driver but a farmer who competed in motor racing.) His old friend, John Coombs, however, amply illustrated Jack's canny farming instincts when he laughingly remarked that whenever he telephoned Jack to offer him a drive Jack always asked "How much?".

Having established that he wanted to become a farmer, in 1950 Jack was sent on a two-year course to The Royal Agricultural College at Cirencester in the Cotswolds. As Cirencester did not demand any university degrees Jack could skip the university route, as Stanley Sears envisaged that Jack would eventually run his own farm or take over the family farm.

This was one of the happiest periods in Jack's life. He lived in student accommodation at Bledisloe Lodge in the village of Coates, sharing a room with Norfolk farmer's son David Simmons, who was to become a life-long friend. Indeed, Simmons was best man at Jack's wedding to his first wife Cicely and Jack was Simmons' best man in turn. After visiting David Simmons' family farm during his college days, and his six months at Spalding, Jack became convinced that he wanted to farm in East Anglia.

At around the same time, 1950, a local farmer called Fred Riches, who farmed on an old airfield at Snetterton, was approached by a Norfolk motor racing enthusiast and restaurant owner called Oliver Sear (no relation). Riches had been able to buy the entire Snetterton airfield, including the runways, from the Ministry of Defence, a very unusual deal in those days because the MoD normally only let out the land it owned in case it needed to use the airfield again.

Oliver Sear asked Riches what he was doing with the Tarmac perimeter roads of the airfield and was told that they were used as tractor access to the farmland. Sear offered to turn the Tarmac into money by using it as the basis of a motor racing circuit. The idea of making money immediately caught Fred Riches' attention and the pair went into business. Oliver Sear obtained planning permission for the track and Snetterton opened as a racing circuit in October 1951, becoming Jack Sears' home motor racing circuit once he moved into Uphall Grange at Ashill, only a few miles away.

The Snetterton Motor Racing Club was formed and its first President was Sir William Bunbury, with Jack Sears as a

Jack Sears has lived for more than 50 years at Uphall Grange in Norfolk. (Jack Sears Archive)

GENTLEMAN JACK

Jack in action at Silverstone with the TT Sunbeam once raced by Dario Resta. (Jack Sears Archive)

VSCC racing at Silverstone with the TT Sunbeam. (Jack Sears Archive)

Prescott Hill Climb with the 1914 TT Sunbeam. (Jack Sears Archive)

committee member. The committee meetings were held in Fred Riches' kitchen. Another member of the committee was the artist Cavendish Morton, who later designed the bodywork for a number of Tojeiros and the AC Le Mans car that Jack Sears raced at Le Mans many years later. Morton was also Chief Paddock Marshal at Snetterton.

However, whilst at Cirencester, Jack Sears continued his motor racing but this time, at his father's suggestion, with the 1914 TT Sunbeam in the opening VSCC race meeting at Silverstone in 1951: an Edwardian Handicap event. Jack loved this big green Sunbeam; it was big and powerful and a handful to drive, but probably paved the way for Jack's future success in cars like the AC Cobra which was also big, powerful and a handful to drive. Every time Jack raced the TT Sunbeam he got faster and faster, and was often able to beat the handicappers. At that first Silverstone meeting he finished second. Three years later he won the prestigious Pomeroy Trophy for the first time in the same car. "I was always the fastest Edwardian and could beat Sam Clutton in the famous Itala." he says.

For a student at Cirencester College motor racing was an expensive pastime and so Jack gave up ski-ing, which had been another of his passions, and put a Wade supercharger on the MG. At the end of 1951 he decided to sell the car, and, though he did not know it at the time, the 1952 replacement was to be a proper racing sports car, an early Cooper-MG bought in kit form by the Reece cousins, Peter and Jackie, whose family business was Blakes of Liverpool. The car was built up with a simple body and cycle wings, and Jack bought it in March 1952 and raced it for the first time in the Bristol Motor and Light Car Club meeting at Castle Coombe on April Fools' Day. He ran in the six lap sports car race and took second place in the 1500cc Class.

Stanley Sears was running a Jaguar XK120 roadster at

Gentleman Jack

Jack Sears bought the Cooper-MG which had been successfully campaigned by Liverpool driver, Peter Reece, and quickly got used to the handling of this fleet little sports racing car. (Jack Sears Archive)

Drifting the ex-Reece Cooper-MG at Snetterton. (Jack Sears Archive)

the time and, as the Cooper-MG was not much fun on the road, Jack bought the Jaguar from his father and ran it in the London Motor Club 'Little Rally.' With two friends, Walter Grant-Norton and Carl Richardson, he won the team prize. Earlier that year Jack had also borrowed his mother's Vauxhall Velox to compete in the RAC Rally.

By now Jack had left college and embarked on farming in his own right. "As a little boy I enjoyed seeing the baby chickens growing up but as I got older I became less interested as they are rather stupid creatures anyhow. My father said he was quite happy to sell the farm and concentrate on his engineering interest with Allen." That decision made, the Sussex farm was sold.

It was now 1952, and Jack had heard that his present farm, Uphall Grange, was coming up for sale. By pure chance the widow of the vicar at Bolney was a great friend of Jack's mother, and they often had tea together. In the course of one conversation the subject came up that Jack was looking for a farm in East Anglia. The lady then said that her sister, a Mrs McLaren, wanted to sell her farm in Norfolk, and why didn't Jack and his father go and see it?

1952, however, was proving a difficult year for the family. Jack's father, Stanley, had to deal with a multitude of problems when his mother, Caroline Sears, died. Caroline Sears was the major shareholder in the Sears company which owned True-Form and Freeman Hardy and Willis, between which there were over nine hundred retail outlets. However, provision had not been made to avoid the punishing death duties that prevailed in Britain at that time, and the duties on Mrs Sears' estate were such that it created an enormous problem for the board. The majority of her shares in the company had to be sold and the buyer was an up-and-coming entrepreneur called Charles Clore. The purchase of the shares in John Sears and Company was his biggest acquisition up to that point, and gave him the notion of creating an empire within the shoe industry. Clore formed the British Shoe Corporation and, in time, bought out some of the most famous shoe companies in Britain, such as Manfield, Dolcis, Lilley & Skinner, and Saxone. When he came to form an overall holding company for his enterprises, Charles Clore decided to use the Sears name and formed Sears Holdings Ltd; a company with no link whatsoever with the Sears family.

Clearly, the Sears family was not left penniless, as various trusts had been set up for the children, but it was a considerable financial blow, nevertheless.

John Sears, Stanley's brother, inherited the family home, Collingtree Grange, but didn't want to live in it. He wanted to farm and so sold the Grange and Park to an aspiring property developer called Bernard Sunley, although he kept the farm which he ran for a number of years. The tragedy was that Sunley immediately pulled down this grand old family house and replaced it with a housing development. Years later, on the death of John Sears, the gardens and farm were converted into a successful golf course and remain as such today.

Jack Starts Racing

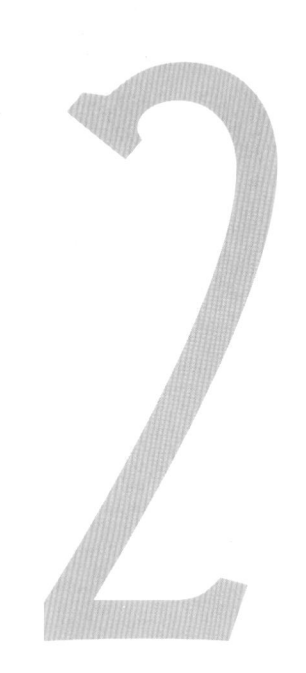

Upon the sale of the main holdings in the family shoe business, Stanley Sears bought Uphall Grange farm in Norfolk. Jack moved into Uphall in the spring of 1953, where he has lived and farmed ever since. Later, in 1953, a year after his grandmother died, Jack Sears and Cicely were married. Some of the beautiful antique furniture from Collingtree Grange was also moved into the new house. Jack Sears never met his grandfather, who died long before he was born, but he remembers his father talking about growing up in the big house at Collingtree Grange.

Jack's grandfather was a close friend of businessman Wenham Joseph Bassett-Lowke; perhaps best loved by children for his famous model railway trains rather than his rather avant-garde lifestyle, which embraced considerable travel around the world, writing and politics. He was a confirmed Fabian, very much to the left of centre of society at that time, and the house he built was based on the style of his friend, the Scottish architect Charles Rennie Mackintosh. As a result of this friendship Jack's father, Stanley, used to be given all the latest model trains to play with. Later, Jack's grandfather was invited by Bassett-Lowke to become chairman, a position he retained until his death in 1916 at the age of just 46.

In 1953 Jack Sears was a newly-married man, settling into his own farm, which meant he gave motor sport a miss that year. There were lots of things to do at Uphall Grange; the previous owner had been 75 and Jack was faced with a lot of tidying up to do as well as planning how the property would be farmed and what would be grown.

By this time the Jaguar XK120 roadster had been replaced by a Jaguar XK120 Fixed-Head Coupé, and in 1954 the lure of motor sport brought Jack back into competition; luckily for Jack, his wife, Cicely, was just as enthusiastic as he was. On March 26 he took the 1914 TT Sunbeam to Silverstone for the opening meeting of the season and came away with the Pomeroy Trophy, an award he had been aiming for and of which he was particularly proud.

However, behind the scenes other things were occurring. Not far from Jack's farm another former Cooper-MG owner called Brian Lister had started to build a very fast Lister-MG sports car with the chassis number BHL1: the first true Lister. The car initially appeared on April 3 1954 at Snetterton, driven by a young Scot called Archie Scott Brown. The races were simply two five lap sprints and Scott Brown won both of them. Brian Lister's plan was to complete a full racing season with the car, so the Snetterton event was simply a warm-up for the British Empire Trophy race at Oulton Park a week later. But what a difference a week can make ...

Archie was third fastest in his Class in practice but a complaint was made to the stewards about Archie's fitness to hold a competition licence. When the stewards saw that his right arm stopped roughly at his elbow and he had only a stump for a hand they withdrew his competition licence and that was that. Ken Wharton took Archie's place for the Empire Trophy meeting, but who was going to drive the car in later events if Archie could not get back his licence? The answer came from Archie Scott Brown who suggested that the young Norfolk driver, Jack Sears, would make a good substitute. So, eight days after Oulton Park, it was Jack Sears who raced the Lister-MG at Brands Hatch and continued to race the car until Archie Scott Brown eventually had his licence restored. Sears, however, was given more drives in the car.

Says Jack: "I met Archie through the Cambridge

An early event in Jack Sears' career; a Goodwood sprint with his Jaguar XK120 Fixed Head Coupé road car. (Jack Sears Archive)

The Vintage Sports Car Club was always dear to Jack Sears' heart, and he raced many of his father's cars at its events. Here he is in the centre of the picture with the replica TT Sunbeam. (Jack Sears Archive)

GENTLEMAN JACK

When Archie Scott-Brown temporarily lost his racing licence he recommended to Brian Lister that Jack Sears drive his factory Lister-MG. (Jack Sears Archive)

University Motor Club when he was sprinting with his MG TD. My father was also a keen member of the club and he and I used to go along to its famous dinner followed, the next day, by a speed trial at Bedwell Hey, and this is how I got to know Archie.

"I always marvelled at the way Archie drove and then, through him, I met Brian Lister This, in turn, led to my meeting Bill Black, who suggested we buy one of the first Lister-Bristols. Bill would do the speed trials and hill climbs with it and I would do the races. So I sold the Jaguar XK120 Coupé to finance my half share in the Lister-Bristol."

Jack drove the works Lister-MG a total of five times in 1954, his best placing being fastest in practice at Brands and second in the 1500cc Class. However, at the international meeting at Snetterton in August, he achieved a more satisfying result, finishing third in his Class to Kenneth McAlpine in the factory Connaught, and John Coombs in his Lotus IX-Connaught. Little did he know that in future years Coombs would be his entrant in a number of events.

During 1954, Jack also got a taste of continental rallying when sharing an Alvis 3 litre on the Tulip Rally in Holland with Bill Banks. Bill was well known in motor sport as a rally driver, and came to realise that there was a business opportunity for him in taking on the British distributorship of a newly-developed adjustable shock absorber, manufactured by the Dutch company Koni. Banks built up a very successful business through Koni, and his son, Warwick Banks, became one of Britain's most promising racing drivers. Bill, however,

Setting off on his first foreign international rally, the Tulip in Holland, Jack peers from the back seat of Bill Banks' Alvis. (Jack Sears Archive)

was actually a farmer who farmed extensively in Lincolnshire and gave Jack the opportunity to co-drive on the Tulip, his first major rally. (It is true that the previous year Jack had run his mother's Vauxhall Velox on the International RAC Rally but the Tulip Rally in an Alvis was much more momentous.)

In 1953 Bill Banks had won the Tulip Rally driving his Bristol 401, and so was one of the favourites in 1954 with the 3 litre Alvis Grey Lady. The plan was that Bill Banks would do all the high-speed sections and all the races and Jack would drive between the stages. Charlotte Sadler was the third member of the crew and did all of the navigation. As it turned out they finished sixth overall and second in their Class. This event triggered Jack's interest in major international rallying and, two years later, he was invited to become a member of the fledgling BMC rally team and was a factory rally driver for BMC for four seasons.

Although rally driving had not yet played a prominent role in Jack Sears' motor sport experience, the 1955 season opened with the RAC International Rally in which Jack – driving a tiny Renault 750 – was entered by the Renault dealer in Norwich, Boshier and Pattenden. Jack was a regular customer at the garage with first his Jaguar XK120 roadster and then the Jaguar XK120 Coupe, and so knew the owner. Stanley Boshier, who was the working partner in the business, had raced, and was a member of the British Racing Drivers Club. His sales director was Tony Hind, well known in British club rallying at the time. Boshier persuaded Renault UK Ltd, to loan a car for Tony Hind to drive on the RAC rally that year. "I was thrilled to be asked to drive with Tony, but the car was absolutely standard. It was a normal showroom car and was prepared by Boshier and Pattenden for the rally." remembers Jack.

The 2 litre Lister-Bristol that replaced Jack's Cooper-MG for sports car racing. (Jack Sears Archive)

Back then there were no off-road special stages (these began in 1960), but the event still had a punishing schedule, particularly as it snowed heavily that year. It is hard to appreciate today that, in those days, a car such as a Renault 750 had difficulty averaging the required 30mph on the road sections, particularly on the Yorkshire Moors or in the Lake District. The event was usually decided on road penalties and the times achieved on a number of driving tests at various towns and cities around Britain. However, Jack and Tony Hind finished second in Class 1, pipped to the post by Keith Ballisat in a Triumph.

During 1954, when driving for Brian Lister, Jack was a witness to the development of the first Lister-Bristol that was being built for Archie Scott Brown. When launched in July 1954 the Lister-Bristol and Archie Scott Brown began to sweep the board. At the end of the year Brian Lister decided to build some customer cars using the information from the Lister-Bristol prototype, and around seven were built for 1955, including one for Bill Black and Jack Sears – chassis BHL 4, registered 4 CNO – one of three Lister-Bristols fitted with a futuristic body designed by Thom Lucas. The car was notable in having inward-curving rear tail fins. The other two Lucas-bodied cars were bought by John Issard-Davies and John Green.

Progressing to more serious British racing at a national level with the Lister-Bristol, Jack felt he had to get himself organised so bought a Standard Vanguard pick-up and trailer with which to travel around the circuits that season.

Jack drove the Lister for the first time at Snetterton in March 1955 where he finished second in the Class. His next event, the British Empire Trophy at Oulton Park two weeks later, helped to truly establish Jack Sears as a racer. In the heat for cars up to 2.7 litres Archie Scott Brown in the factory Lister-Bristol secured pole position with Jack just 0.2 of a

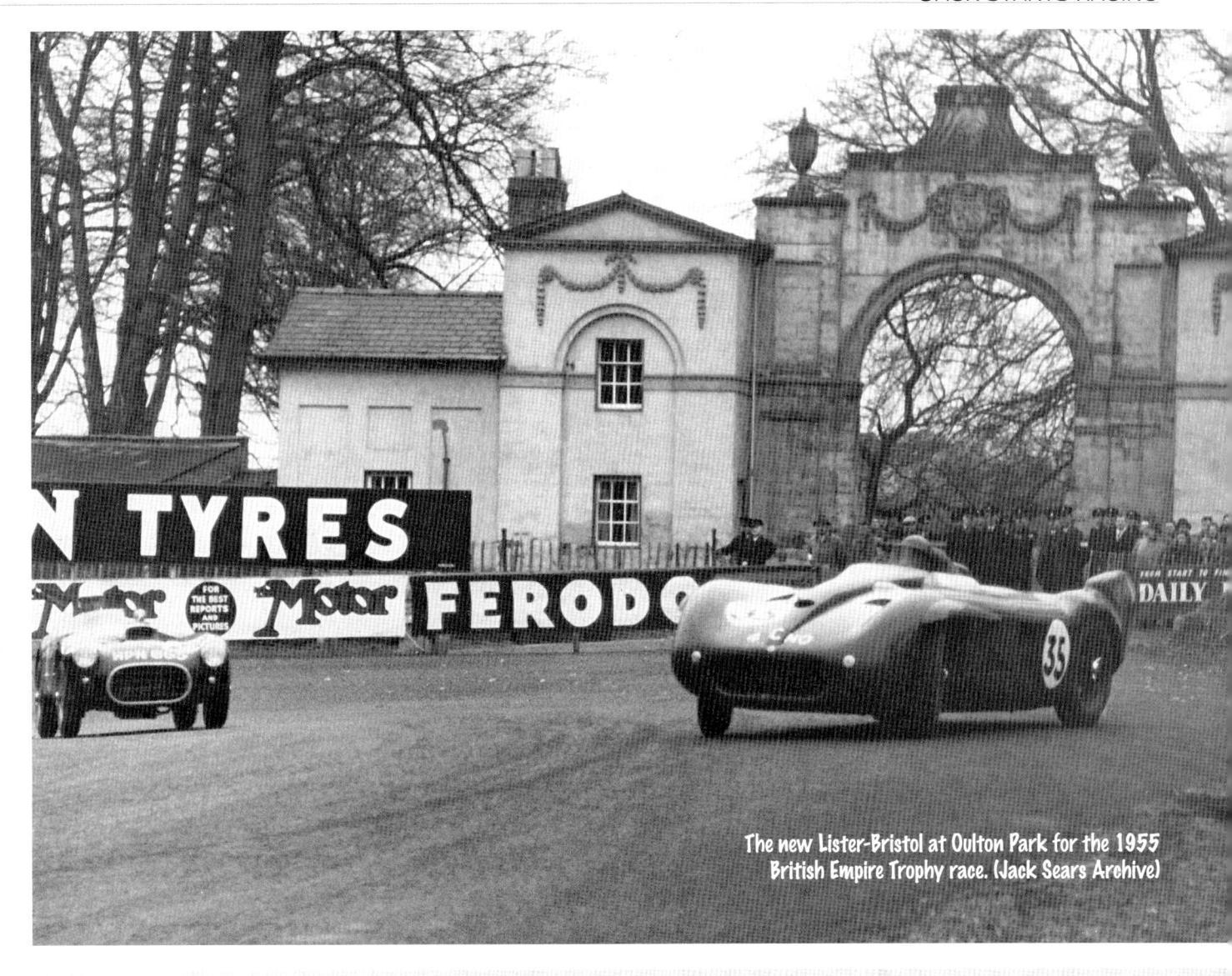

JACK STARTS RACING

The new Lister-Bristol at Oulton Park for the 1955 British Empire Trophy race. (Jack Sears Archive)

Jack Sears, in the 2 litre Lister-Bristol at Snetterton, holds off his friend, Archie Scott Brown, in the factory Lister-Bristol. (Jack Sears Archive)

On the line: Jack Sears on his second outing with the Lister-Bristol at Oulton Park. (Jack Sears Archive)

second behind him, and Reg Parnell in the Aston Martin in third. Jack had problems in the races, however, and managed 5th place only in his Class.

In mid-season Jack had his first major motor racing accident at Silverstone: he was racing the Lister-Bristol and went flying off the road. When he hit the bank the car overturned and Jack was lucky to get off with a bruised shoulder. "Two things happened, really. I was going a bit too fast into Club Corner and, for some reason, the engine was tending to miss; just when I needed the power it went flat and the car slid across the grass and hit the high earth bank. Willie Green had a similar accident at the Goodwood Revival Meeting in 2005; in Willie's case, the Maserati landed on top of him but, in my case, I was thrown out and landed alongside the car: I was a very lucky boy."

Jack decided to sell the Lister-Bristol which then began a long journey through many owners. Northern enthusiast Frank Elliot owned and raced the car extensively before selling it and buying a Costin Lister-Jaguar (the ex-Jonathan Seiff car). Elliot was killed in this car the first time he drove it, testing at Thornaby. The Lister-Bristol was sold by a dealer to Peter Jackson from Whitby who raced it until 1984. He says: "That year I had a heart attack at Silverstone when racing the Lister-Bristol and was lucky not to destroy the car. I then sold it to a Finnish tea importer who came over to collect it. I received payment in an envelope full of £20 notes."

Today, the same Lister-Bristol is owned by Dr Barry Wood, who lives in Scotland and races his car in historic races all over Britain. Ironically, Barry loaned the car to my son, Lance Gauld, who raced it for the first time in the 2006 Silverstone Classic event, winning the 2 litre Class with Tony Wood.

Success with the Lister certainly brought Jack Sears'

Silverstone start: Roy Salvadori (Aston Martin DB3S) disappears out of the picture followed by Jack Sears (Lister-Bristol), Jim Russell (Manx Cooper), and Tony Brooks (Frazer-Nash Le Mans Replica). (Jack Sears Archive)

name to the fore and he received a telephone call from Peter Reece, who had sold Jack his Cooper-MG two years before. Peter had been chosen to join the newly-formed British Motor Corporation competitions department and become a rally driver. Recalling the moment, Jack Sears remembers his response: "'Gosh, that's fantastic, what a stroke of luck for you.' He then said his first event was the Monte Carlo Rally in 1956, and would I be his co-driver? The car was going to be an Austin A50 saloon with an MG engine and a floor-mounted gearchange which would run in the Specials Class and would be quite a little hot rod. I said, 'That's a huge honour Peter, definitely, I will come.'"

Full of excitement Jack put down the phone, but his pleasure was shortlived as, just a few weeks later, he received another telephone call to say that Peter Reece had been killed in a road accident. "This was devastating news for me because Peter was such a helluva nice guy. Archie Scott Brown also knew Peter and so Archie and I decided to go to the funeral together. I drove to Cambridge to meet Archie and we drove to Liverpool. I had never been driven very far by Archie, perhaps up and down to the pub, and this was my first long distance drive with him. I was amazed at the way Archie drove; the car control, the smoothness.

"Archie was a very heavy smoker and, bearing in mind he only had one hand, he would stick his stump on the steering wheel, flip open the cigarette packet with his left hand, flick a lighter and carry on smoking: all this at about 70mph in his Ford Zephyr. I felt totally happy about that because everything was under control.

"After the funeral we were all invited back to Blakes of Liverpool, the Reece family Ford dealership. I had never met Peter's father, Stanley Blake Reece, but somebody came up to me and asked if Archie and I would go up to the office and see 'SB', as Peter's father was called.

Old friends and rivals. Henry Taylor, driving the Murkett Brothers' D-Type Jaguar (later raced by Jim Clark), takes a tighter line into Club Corner at Silverstone than Jack Sears in the Lister-Bristol. (Jack Sears Archive)

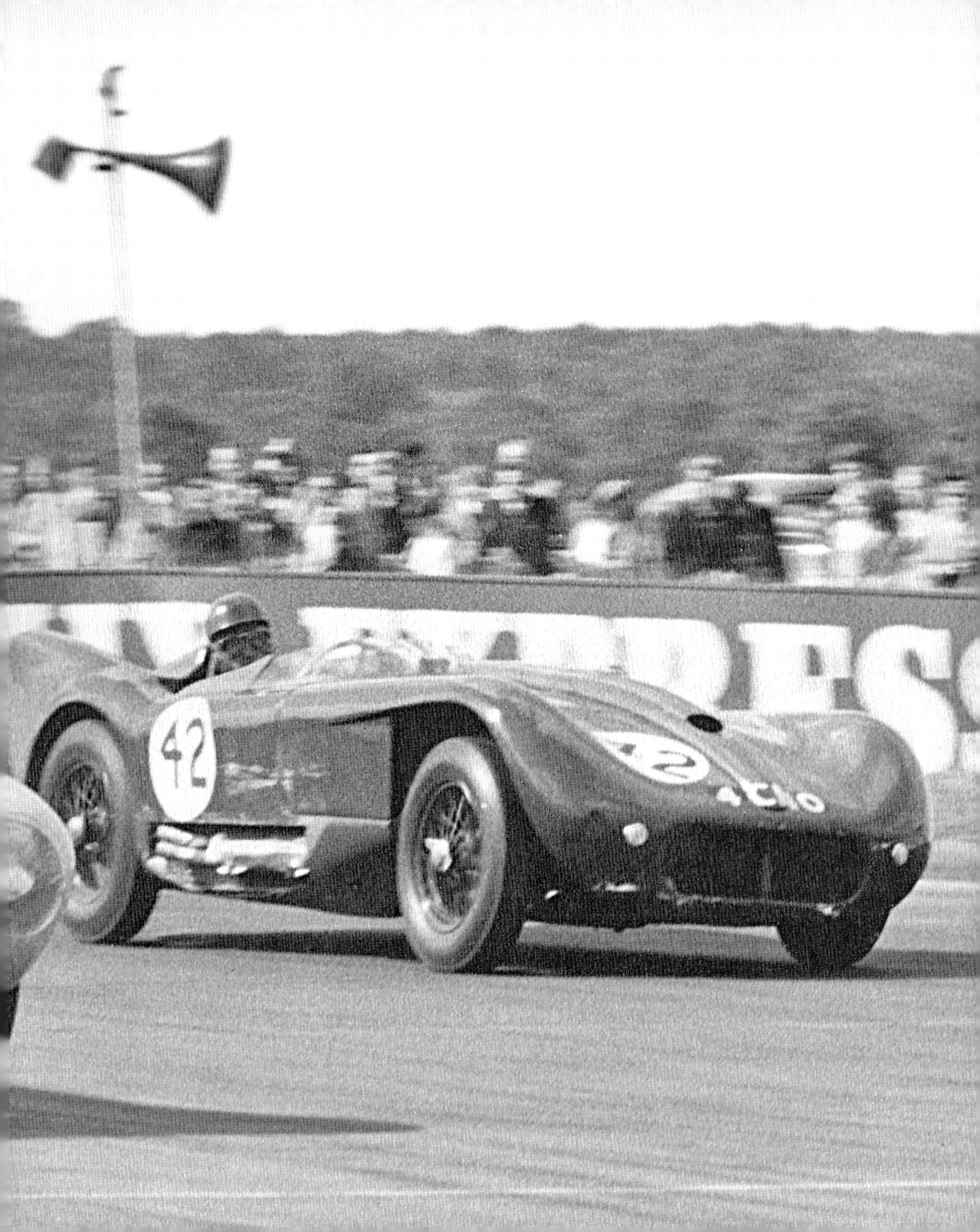
42

GENTLEMAN JACK

At Goodwood Her Majesty, Queen Elizabeth II, hands over a trophy to Jack and Cicely Sears in the 1905 Rolls-Royce. (Jack Sears Archive)

"We expressed our sympathy to him as Peter was his only son. Suddenly, he said 'Jack, I know you were going with Peter on the Monte Carlo Rally. I have been in touch with Marcus Chambers, the new BMC competitions manager, and told him I want the car to run for Peter's sake. I want you to take it over and also I want Archie to go with you.' Well, Archie's eyes opened wide. Mr Reece turned to him and said 'Well, you'll go, won't you?'. Archie said he was not a good rally driver but that, yes, Mr Reece, he would do it with me.

"Neither Archie nor I was great at navigation so we needed a navigator, and Marcus Chambers came up with Kenneth Best, who was the competitions manager for National Benzole at the time."

Jack, however, had another problem on the horizon. He and Cicely's first child, David, was born on December 9 1955 just a few short weeks before the Monte Carlo Rally. One of the enduring factors in Jack's life was that his wife always encouraged and gave him every support in his racing and rallying, and told him she didn't mind him doing the event despite the circumstances. By then, however, David had been christened, with Archie Scott Brown and *Autocar* sports editor Peter Garnier as his godfathers.

Come January 1956 and Jack, Archie and Ken Best set off for Lisbon, from where they were due to start the Monte, which, in those days, lasted for three non-stop days and nights.

JACK STARTS RACING

it was decided to drive straight to Nice, have some lunch and clock in at Monte Carlo at what would have been their exact check-in time. As the other competitors were still on the Mountain Circuit they got into Nice and parked the battered car in front of a restaurant. The proprietor was stunned when the three British drivers walked in and coolly ordered lunch; pretty soon the bar at the restaurant began to fill up with enthusiasts attracted by the battered rally car outside.

After lunch they continued to Monte Carlo and clocked in at exactly the correct time, which made it seem as if they had completed the event in this battered car and arrived on time. They received a big cheer and quite a lot of press interest but, of course, as soon as they handed over their road book the organisers realised half of it was missing as they hadn't been to the controls. They were dismissed but at least they had honoured Marcus Chambers' mandate to get the car to the finish. As it turned out they still classified as finishers in the event in the position they held at the end of the original road sections.

The Austin A50 and crew went well on the event and finished 49th overall on arrival at Monaco, which meant they qualified for the final punishing 'mountain circuit', with all the regular special stages, including the notorious Col de Turini. Elated at having qualified, the crew decided that Archie Scott Brown would be the man to tackle this last series of special stages over the mountains. Eye witnesses have testified that, by this time, Archie was far from happy and did not enjoy being a passenger on the snow and ice. He was still game, however, as all agreed he was the fastest of the three of them. About a third of the way through, and on the downside of the Col de Turini, Archie suddenly cried out that he didn't think he could stop. "There was a right-hand bend ahead of us and the brakes had seriously faded so Archie threw the car sideways. There was no snow on that bit but the road was damp and icy, and though the car was slowing down it just teetered off the edge, turned on its roof and wedged against a tree. We all shouted to each other to see everyone was ok and crawled out to survey the damage. Now, as far as BMC competitions manager, Marcus Chambers, was concerned, no matter what happened on an event you had to bring the car home." laughs Jack.

The threesome felt that, if they could get the Austin back on its wheels and onto the road, it was probably driveable. At this, out of the blackness, a large crowd of Frenchmen suddenly appeared and, taking in the situation, pitched in to help push the car on its roof like a toboggan further down the slope to a track where it was lifted back onto its wheels. There was no windscreen but the team checked the oil, got inside and lay on their backs to prise up the roof with their feet to give some headroom, then managed to drive the car up the track and back onto the road. However, by now, they were out of the rally as they had lost so much time, so

During 1956 Jack Sears did very little on the motor racing front as he continued as a member of the BMC factory rally team. This was fortunate for him as this year was a pivotal one for Great Britain, which went to war with Egypt over nationalisation of the Suez Canal. This introduced many restrictions, petrol rationing and, in November, a total ban on motor racing. Thankfully, by that time the racing season was over anyway and so the ban had a minimal effect.

Indeed, the only car Jack raced during the season was probably the oddest he ever had: the FCB that he ran three times at Snetterton. Built by Sir William (Bill) Bunbury and some friends, the car was unusual in that it had a wooden body and a Standard 10 engine. It was not a world-beater but Jack did have a sprint Class win with it at Snetterton. However, when Oliver Sear created the Snetterton circuit, Bill Bunbury was appointed Chief Steward and became President of the Snetterton Motor Racing Club.

One winter's evening at a dinner party, Jack Sears met a young motor engineer and former farm pupil called Mike McKee, who was working for the Mann Egerton dealership in Norwich, and was proud of his Jaguar XK120 roadster.

The McKee family originally came from Scotland but settled in Norfolk where Mike's great grandfather and grandfather were doctors. Mike's father, Kenneth McKee, was a surgeon working in Norwich General Hospital.

31

For 25 years Ken McKee worked with John Watson Farrar, and the two were responsible for development of the McKee-Farrar ball and socket joint for hip and knee surgery. Such joints already existed but the McKee-Farrar joint was made of alloy which was cemented into the existing bone structure with plastic, and overcame the problem of durability that the original stainless steel versions demonstrated. As he had lived in Norwich during the war, Kenneth McKee had seen how aircraft pilots had their hips smashed through hitting the dashboards during a crash, so he decided to work in the field of artificial joints. By the time McKee retired he had replaced more than 1000 hip joints and been made Honorary Doctor of Science at Cambridge. As Mike McKee recalls: "My father was famous throughout the world, and in the 1960s trainloads of surgeons would travel to Norwich to watch him operate."

During their conversation at dinner Mike McKee regaled Jack with an account of the road accidents he had been involved in whilst driving his Jaguar XK120, to which Sears replied that it would be much more sensible if Mike did his fast driving on a race track and not on the roads. McKee asked how to get started in racing and Sears told him about a Jaguar Drivers Club race meeting due to be held at Snetterton the following weekend. Mike McKee went back to Mann Eggerton and took his Jaguar to the tuning department to check the brakes. He duly turned up at Snetterton where Jack Sears introduced him to everyone. McKee borrowed a crash helmet and went out for his first race: "I was very lucky and won two races that day. In one of them I was leading the Club President, who was driving an immaculate XK120 Fixed-Head Coupe against my rather tatty XK120 roadster, and he tried to come up on my inside on Norwich Straight but his brakes were not good enough and he shot into the bank. I felt sorry for him with that beautiful car."

Mike McKee became one of the most successful Formula Junior drivers of the 1960s, finishing third in the British Championship behind Jim Clark and Trevor Taylor. He won the *Motor Sport* Brooklands Memorial Trophy in his ex-Mike Taylor Lotus II, and enjoyed a successful career in racing that included a test for BRM and factory drives for Elva.

From then on McKee and Sears became close friends, and Mike was instrumental in introducing Jack to his second wife, Diana. Also, on two future occasions, Jack Sears was to call upon the professional services of Ken McKee, particularly after his career-ending accident in a Lotus 40 at Silverstone in 1965.

Jack had a relatively quiet 1957 and raced his own Austin A105 in a number of saloon car events, as this was before the advent of a British saloon championship. More often than not, he won his Class against cars such as the Ford Zephyr, but was concerned when he was beaten at Silverstone by John Webb driving a Jensen 541 which was really more of a GT car than a saloon. In those days if it had a roof it became a saloon.

Towards the end of the season the Borgward company, which was trying to establish its new Borgward Isabella in the British market, decided to attempt a high-speed, 24 hour run round Snetterton. Jack Sears was asked to join fellow drivers Tommy Bridger, Mike McKee, Brian Fry and Tony Hind, and they completed the 24 hour run at an average of 62mph, including all stops, which was a remarkable performance. Later, Tommy Bridger was to race an Isabella TS in British saloon car racing.

By 1958 the Suez affair that had curtailed racing the year before was long forgotten, and Jack prepared for the Monte Carlo Rally with an Austin A105, partnered by Sam Moore and his old friend Ken Best. It was not a success as that year the Monte Carlo Rally was almost decimated by heavy snow in the Alps. Jack and his crew were eliminated when they accumulated over an hour's lateness due to the snow.

Two months later Jack appeared on the RAC Rally driving an Austin Healey 100/6 for the first time. This car had been fitted with disc brakes and a new, six-port cylinder head for more power. His friend, Peter Garnier, co-drove with him but they experienced a lot of trouble and finished well down the field.

During the year Nobby Spero, a great stalwart of the historic racing movement, offered Jack a drive with the ex-Whitney Straight Maserati. "Nobby had got to the point where he didn't think he was going fast enough. He suggested that I raced the Maserati in the all-comers scratch race at the VSCC meeting at Silverstone in April. I was racing the Sunbeam TT at the same meeting, and the Clerk of the Course gave clearance for me to take Nobby's place. It was the first single-seater grand prix car I ever raced so I did my practice and went on to the grid alongside Bill Moss in his ERA, who was fastest. It was an interesting car to drive as it had a Wilson pre-selector gearbox which I was able to master quite quickly; I finished second to the ERA."

Meanwhile, on the rallying trail things were happening at BMC. Team manager Marcus Chambers finally convinced the board that they should concentrate on the Austin Healey 100/6 as it was the car most likely to take outright rally wins. This led to a lot of work behind the scenes.

The real problem was the successful Triumph TRs, which were nimble and – despite their 2 litre engines – very competitive. By contrast the Healey was a big truck of a car that had a habit of losing its exhaust system whenever the going got tough. Over 80 per cent of the big Healeys produced were being sold in the United State, which should have given everyone a clue: the car needed to be better prepared for the loose-surfaced, rougher rally roads encountered in the European Touring Championship.

JACK STARTS RACING

With his newfound freedom to develop the rally team, Marcus Chambers decided to enlist the engineering talent of the MG division, and asked Alec Hounslow, Syd Enever and Terry Mitchell to suggest ideas to improve the Healey's handling. Syd Enever came up with the solution in the time-honoured 'blue sky' tradition. The story goes that he was at Oxford railway station and noticed that the wheel sets that carried the railway carriages were simply controlled by massive leaf springs with no form of shock absorber. He went to the library and read all the books about railway engineering, and in one found a paragraph which stated that friction between the leaves of springs damped oscillations, obviating need for shock absorbers. If it worked on a railway train, would it work on a car, he wondered? The end result was fourteen-leaf rear springs for the Healey that were so rigid the team could carry a larger fuel tank and a couple of spare wheels without the car dragging its tail along the road. There was a legacy, however; a marked tail-snapping oversteer that was tamed by various different roll bars.

All this was completed in time for the Alpine Rally of 1958, a tough event by any standards. The rally brought no great results, save for an Alpine Cup courtesy of Scotsmen Bill Shepherd and John Williamson for finishing seventh overall, but this had little to do with the handling of the car. John Gott, for example, lost a wheel due to a faulty hub, Pat Moss ran the bearings in her car when someone tied a knot in the oil breather pipe (!), and Jack Sears won at Monza. In the event he finished 5th in Class and 11th overall. He made fastest time over five laps of the J P Wimille circuit at Marseille, this being the final test.

However, it was Jack's performance at Monza which indicated to Marcus Chambers that Healey was now on the right track and the Austin Healey 100/6 had been transformed into a potential rally winner. At the Liège-Rome-Liège rally this was further underlined when Pat Moss finished a fantastic fourth overall and BMC won the manufacturers' team prize.

Jack Sears raced just two single-seater cars in his career; one was the UDT-Laystall Cooper-Climax and the other, seen here, was Nobby Spero's ex-Whitney Straight Maserati. (Jack Sears Archive)

The 1959 Alpine Rally. Jack – with Sam Moore – retired with the fan through the radiator of this factory Austin-Healey 3000. (Courtesy Junior: Jack Sears Archive)

JACK STARTS RACING

Alpine Rally 1959: Sears and Sam Moore on one of the special stages. (Courtesy Junior: Jack Sears Archive)

The Silverstone test on the 1960 RAC Rally. Jack finished 4th overall and won the *Motor Sport* Trophy. (Jack Sears Archive)

35

British Saloon Car Champion

The first British Saloon Car Championship was launched in 1958 and run on a Class basis; unlike today when all the cars run in the same Class. Marcus Chambers immediately saw the promotional and sales potential of winning this championship with an Austin, and so it was arranged that Jack Sears would personally buy an Austin A105 for the series. The Austin's main opposition came from Tommy Sopwith and Sir Gawaine Baillie in the Equipe Endeavour Mark I, 3.4 litre Jaguars. As the Austin and the Jaguars were in different Classes, Jack had to ensure that he won his Class at every race.

He started out well but, as the season progressed, it became obvious that there might be a tie for the title, a possibility that the British Racing and Sports Car Club had not considered. Not every race counted in the championship and so drivers could drop their two poorest results. During the early part of the season Jack had been beaten in the Class by Jeff Uren driving a Mark II Ford Zephyr fitted with a Raymond Mays, three-carburettor cylinder head. This prompted Marcus Chambers to think about how to get more performance out of the Austin. The BMC Competitions Department was not equipped to do this in the time necessary, so he approached John Sprinzel, George Hulbert and Graham Hill at Speedwell Engineering and asked them to design a three-carburettor cylinder head in a hell of a hurry. Speedwell – thanks to Hulbert's skill – had a great reputation for its work with Austin A35s and so was well known to BMC. Speedwell set everything aside and produced the three-carburettor head that gave an immediate increase in performance. Despite the fact that Jack Sears actually owned the Austin A105, it was the BMC Competitions Department that paid for the design and production of the cylinder head.

The new head put Jack back on a winning streak and he began to catch up on Sopwith. Dropping his two lowest finishes was to Jack Sears' advantage as Tommy Sopwith in his Jaguar had been beaten only once (by Mike Hawthorn) so had to drop a win. But what was going to happen if they tied?

Says Jack: "It was put to us by the BRSCC that it looked likely there would be a dead heat if we both won our Classes in the final round at Brands Hatch, so could we decide the issue by spinning a coin? Tommy and I couldn't believe what we were hearing. I remember I said something along the lines that I had not raced all year to have the bloody championship decided on the spin of a coin!

"I said I would not agree to that and Tommy said the same so we told them to have another think. What they came up with was very interesting. They contacted Marcus Chambers, explained the situation and asked him about supplying two identical cars so that there could be a run-off between Tommy and me. My racing Austin 105 had been used on rallies as well as racing, and Marcus sold it to me prior to this 1958 season so that I could race it as a private entry. The fact that he looked after it mechanically at his expense was another thing but it was registered in my name, I entered it and it was not a BMC entry."

Marcus Chambers offered to prepare two rally Riley 1.5s to be used for a match race at Brands Hatch should the need arise.

Jack continues: "Obviously, Tommy and I were asked if we agreed to this and we both said it was a good way of sorting it out. Well, we both practised in the cars and predictably one was a little quicker than the other. So then it was a question of who drove which car first. There were

The first car to win the British Saloon Car Championship was this Austin A105, driven by Jack Sears in 1958. (Jack Sears Archive)

A wet Brands Hatch, and Jack Sears, in his Austin A105, battles with John Webb's Jensen, followed by Alan Hutchinson's Riley 1.5. (Jack Sears Archive)

Gentleman Jack

Alan Adler with his Austin A105 gets sideways, eventually overturning in the saloon car race at Silverstone in 1958. Jack Sears is safely ahead of him in his Austin A105. (Jack Sears Archive)

Silverstone 1957 and Jack Sears with his Austin A105 saloon waves Tommy Sopwith, partly hidden, through, whilst Mike Hawthorn waits to pounce in his MkI 3.4 litre Jaguar. (Jack Sears Archive)

no numbers on the Rileys so BRSCC decided that one car would race with its headlights on and the other with the headlights off to make it easier to recognise who was in which car. So that was the package.

"In the actual saloon car race I was fastest in my Class and Tommy was fastest in his Class. So now we had to face the run-off and they did it immediately, they didn't wait until the end of the race meeting. So the two BMC mechanics drove the two Rileys round to the start line and Tommy and I were standing there looking at each other, thinking 'this is showdown time.' There was tremendous tension, it was like a shoot-out, walking down the street with the six-guns out. We did spin a coin for choice of car knowing that one car was faster than the other. Tommy won the toss so I knew he had the faster car and would beat me. I had no hang-ups about that, it was just a question of trying to keep as close to him as I possibly could. Quite predictably he won the first five lap race.

"We got out the cars and I remember walking round to the other car in the wet, taking a rag out of my pocket and wiping the soles of my feet before getting into the car. I made an excellent start and led into Paddock Bend so he had to keep up with me. We didn't get any pit signals so it was just a question of going for it in pouring rain. Those little Riley 1.5s were really good with their beefed-up suspension and shock absorbers. Finally, the chequered flag came down and on the slowing down lap I remember wondering if I had done enough as it was difficult to judge visually. When they announced the aggregate times I had beaten Tommy by just 1.6 seconds. So I became British Saloon Car Champion for 1958 and won the princely sum of £100! Indeed, my entire winnings from motor racing in 1958, including television appearances, came to £837.5s".

(As recently as 2004, a friend of Jack's, Martin Thomas, who used to race a Chevrolet Camaro, telephoned him to say he had found the 1958 championship-winning Austin in a barn. He recognised the registration number TOL563 and saw it was a wreck. Eventually, the Austin and some other derelict cars were brought out of the barn and Martin asked Jack if the car had a three-carburettor head by Speedwell which had been homologated halfway through the 1958 season to keep up with the Ford Zephyrs, which Jack confirmed. Jack originally sold the car at the end of the 1958 season to a garage in East Anglia that knew what it was and kept it for a while. It was later sold and then involved in a serious accident where it was badly damaged. It was in this state that the car was found in the barn but it had been there so long in a damp atmosphere it had almost completely rotted away. Martin, however, managed to find a donor car which was a proper short boot A105 and hopes to re-create TOL563 and race it with all the original parts but in a new body and chassis.)

Jack replaced the Austin A105 with one of the factory Austin-Healey 100/6 rally cars to race in the *Autosport* GT Championship in 1959. (This car is also still around as it was later sold to fellow BMC factory driver, Peter Riley.) The arrangement with Marcus Chambers was the same as with the Austin: BMC would prepare the car but Jack entered it privately. However, halfway through the 1959 season it was re-badged as an Austin-Healey 3000.

Jack's 1959 season was rather leisurely, dominated by GT racing in England with the Austin-Healey and driving officially for BMC in the European Rally Championship. Indeed, the only other events Jack did that year were two races for his friend, Tommy Sopwith, in Equipe Endeavour Jaguar 3.4s, and a VSCC race at Silverstone in the TT Sunbeam.

The first of the Jaguar races was in a 100 mile saloon car race at Snetterton, where Jack led until the disc brake pads wore out and he finished second to Sir Gawaine Baillie in the other Endeavour car. (Sir Gawaine Baillie owned and ran his own car but under the Equipe Endeavour banner.) The other occasion was at the international meeting at Brands Hatch where he won the race in the Jaguar. On both occasions Sears drove one of Sopwith's cars with the registration number 400, a number that Tommy Sopwith always tried to get for his cars. The story is told of the occasion he sent his man to register a Jaguar and specified he wanted a 400 number. When he came back two days later his man told him the number was not 400, at which an exasperated Sopwith complained that, after being asked to get a registration plate with 400, he was now telling him that he hadn't. It took a few more exchanges for Sopwith to realise that the actual registration number was NOT400!

The next event in the European Rally Championship was the Tulip Rally where Jack had one of his regular co-drivers, Peter Garnier, sports editor of *Autocar*. I was competing on the International Tulip Rally that year so was able to watch Jack Sears at his best in a rally car. Sears won the GT Class outright, his farming friends, and later Austin-Healey team mates, the Morley twins, winning the event outright with a Jaguar 3.4. To win the GT Class Sears had beaten the 300 SLs, Aston Martins and Ferraris.

Jack set the fastest race average at Zandvoort during the final tests, and won the Interland Trophy put up for the winning team. The other two drivers in the team were Cuth Harrison with his Ford and Keith Ballisat. "... and I finished up with £36 in my pocket" said Jack.

In September 1959 it was back to the international rally scene and the gruelling Liège-Rome-Liège event which was run non-stop over four days and four nights. It really tested driver and co-driver fitness and also their ability to share the stresses for such a long period. For this event Jack again chose *Autocar* sports editor Peter Garnier as his co-driver.

"I was once told that the Liège organisers had always

RAC Rally 1959, the Austin-Healey team with manager, Marcus Chambers (left), Willie Cave, Jack Sears, and the Morley twins, Donald and Erle. (Jack Sears Archive)

hoped that one day they would not have a single finisher. It never actually happened and I think they meant a finisher who did not exceed the thirty minutes lateness allowance otherwise you were automatically excluded. This was cumulative so that if you were a minute late at one control and two minutes late at the next it meant you were now 3 minutes into your lateness timing.

"We were into the last 24 hours and I cannot remember exactly where we were but the maps indicated that we drove down a valley. When we got to the bottom we found there was no bridge over the river. It was a new road being built and for some reason we missed what might have been said earlier about the road being closed. We had to turn round and come back, following the detour; to this day I do not know how we missed this. When we finally got to the control we had gone over our 30 minutes. I remember shouting at the officials that they should have made it quite clear the road was closed and how were we to know about local knowledge? Then the old story came out with a shrug, the others didn't make that mistake, we were the foolish ones, so they took our road book away and that was that."

At the end of 1959 Jack decided, after four years as a factory driver for BMC, that he was a better racing driver than a rally driver and from then on would concentrate on racing. Marcus Chambers, team manager of BMC, had offered Jack a continuation of his contract into 1960, but Jack explained that he would rather give up the rally side, though if they ever wanted him to race for them they had just to pick up the phone.

Having made that decision Jack began to think about the 1960 season, and here his old friend Tommy Sopwith entered the picture. By now great friends, Jack was always a welcome guest at the little Pimms parties Tommy would hold after each race meeting in his Equipe Endeavour caravan. Sopwith told Jack that he wanted to put Equipe Endeavour on a more professional footing, and run two Mark II 3.8 Jaguars against the John Coombs Jaguars to be driven by Graham Hill and Roy Salvadori. Jack's team mate with Equipe Endeavour was to be Michael Parkes.

Tommy Sopwith and Equipe Endeavour then figured large in Jack Sears' racing life with the Endeavour Mark II Jaguars in touring car racing and an Aston Martin DB4GT in

Jack Sears was one of the original oversteer kings. Here, he demonstrates with Tommy Sopwith's Jaguar 3.8. (Jack Sears Archive)

Drifting Tommy Sopwith's Aston Martin DB4GT in its Equipe Endeavour colours. (Jack Sears Archive)

Drifting the Equipe Endeavour Aston Martin DB4GT lightweight at Aintree. (Jack Sears Archive)

GT events. Also, the first Ferrari raced by Jack Sears was the ex-Rob Walker 1960 TT-winning 250GTSWB (chassis number 2118GT) that Sopwith and Col Ronnie Hoare of Maranello Concessionaires bought for Michael Parkes to race.

Tommy Sopwith was, and still is, one of the true gentleman racing drivers. His father, Sir Thomas Octave Murdock Sopwith, was born in London, the son of a prominent civil engineer, but was to become one of the most famous sportsmen in Britain as well as a pioneer in British aviation. Sir Thomas became captivated by flying when taken to Dover to see John Moisant become the first man to fly a passenger across the English Channel. This inspired him to try flying and at Brooklands he was taken up by Gustav Blondeau in a Farman. He then taught himself to fly and flew for the first time in 1910. Mind you, the flight was short-lived as the plane crashed after just 300 yards! Nonetheless, Tommy Sopwith became the holder of the 31st aviation certificate issued by the Royal Aero Club.

He established his own aircraft company in 1912, and in 1914 his Sopwith Tabloid seaplane – flown by C Howard Pixton – won the Schneider Trophy at Monaco. During the First World War Sopwith made aviation history with his Sopwith Pup and Sopwith Camel aeroplanes. Little credit, then, to the British government, which bankrupted him after the war due to punitive anti-profiteering taxes. However, Sopwith restarted in the aircraft business and named his new company Hawker after his chief engineer, Harry Hawker. Hawker went on to produce a multitude of planes, and once more the Hawker Hurricane was to dominate as the leading British fighter plane in the Second World War, even though the Spitfire got most of the publicity.

Sir Thomas Sopwith – he was knighted in 1953 – led challenges for the Americas Cup with his yachts Endeavour and Endeavour II, and his son, the present Tommy Sopwith, called his racing team Equipe Endeavour after his father's yachts.

Tommy Sopwith was born in 1932 in London, and was evacuated for three years to the United States during the Second World War. At that time his father was Chairman of Hawker-Siddeley, so was fully occupied during the war building Hawker Hurricanes. Tommy was educated at Stowe School, just a few miles from Silverstone, and was keen on cross-country running. When he had the chance to decide where they would run he always chose Silverstone. "I vividly remember watching the first British Grand Prix, with all the great British drivers" he says.

Tommy Sopwith's Sphinx sports car powered by an Armstrong-Siddeley engine. (Jack Sears Archive)

After completing two years' National Service in the Coldstream Guards Tommy was offered a place in New College, Oxford. "I didn't take it, and looking back now I think it was a lunatic decision. I was going to read law and on balance I regret I didn't do that. I worked for some time at Armstrong-Siddeley as a post-graduate apprentice, then I wound up running the experimental department. I then decided I wanted to paddle my own canoe rather than work with a large company of which my father was the Chairman, so I bought a Ford dealership in Brighton.

"The first car I actually raced was a Jaguar XK120 at a members' meeting at Goodwood. However, when I was working at Armstrong-Siddeley I decided it would be a good idea to have a car based on the Armstrong Siddeley Sapphire engine. This was the Sphinx because the Armstrong-Siddeley radiator mascot was a Sphinx.

"I was in a position to have it hotted up inexpensively, and put it into an Allard chassis as it was the most cost-effective way of going about this. This was not an official Armstrong-Siddeley project but a personal thing. In fact, the whole thing fell off the back of a lorry!

"In many ways it was a horrendous car but it beat a number of C-type Jaguars from time to time."

Sopwith had a Cooper-Jaguar, then bought the first customer bobtail Cooper and ran it alongside the factory car raced by Ivor Bueb. He had a bad accident in the Cooper at Oulton Park and parental pressure was such that he decided to retire from serious racing and simply race saloon cars.

"I bought a Mark I 3.4 litre Jaguar; they were sensational cars. You could drive to the circuit, race and then drive back home again. I had a marvellous race at Silverstone with Michael Hawthorn in 1958 at the International Trophy. It was great for someone like me, who never claimed to be an ace Formula 1 driver, to have total confidence in someone you were getting very, very close to. I knew he was not going make a fool of himself so I felt I could do what I liked. It was the most enjoyable race of my life.

"At the end of 1958 I had an interview with my father who very intelligently did not do the heavy-handed bit. He just asked me if I wanted to be world champion. I said 'no', and he replied 'why not?' I told him I did not think I was good enough so he asked me why I bothered."

This, then, was the background to Tommy Sopwith becoming an entrant rather than a competitor. He had run a Mark I Jaguar 3.4 in 1959 but now was going to run a proper two-car Jaguar team.

43

Jack in a hurry driving Tommy Sopwith's Aston Martin DB4GT in Equipe Endeavour colours at Silverstone. (Jack Sears Archive)

Jack had raced one of Sopwith's 3.4s, but in 1960 the Sopwith team was running 3.8 litre Jaguars. The problem with the 3.4 litre Jaguar saloons was that they had a narrow rear track, though this made them spectacular to watch as they slid through the corners on opposite lock. With the 3.8s, however, this had been corrected and the resultant performance hike was considerable. A well prepared racing 3.8 litre Jaguar was capable of close on 140mph, which was quite sensational for a saloon car at that time. Equipe Endeavour also had an Aston Martin DB4GT, but Jack felt the car had to be wrestled round circuits unlike the smoother-handling Jaguar E-type.

Shortly after Jack had agreed to join Sopwith he received a telephone call from Marcus Chambers at BMC asking if he would rejoin the team and race an Austin-Healey 3000 at the 1960 Sebring 12 Hour Race with Peter Riley.

As Jack recalls: "He said he was taking the 3000s to Sebring and would I be available to be one of the works drivers? I telephoned Tommy Sopwith and asked if he would mind if I went off to Sebring. He told me to go off and enjoy it.

"It was my first trip to America and I remember we flew by BOAC Comet to New York where we met a remarkable man, Babe Learoyd, who had been a bomber pilot during the war and had won the Victoria Cross. Babe represented BMC's public affairs department in the United States. He was a real charmer and the fact he had won the VC impressed me as I had never met anybody who had won a VC before."

Peter Riley also remembers the occasion for he had been racing a Lotus VI and later a Series 2 Lotus Eleven at that time. "I was actually head-hunted by Marcus Chambers from Ford where I had been driving Ford Zephyrs in rallies. He knew I was interested in racing and offered me both a rallying and racing contract, and my first event was Sebring."

Jack and Peter Riley flew to Miami and drove the Corvair rental car to the motel in Avon Park, a small township

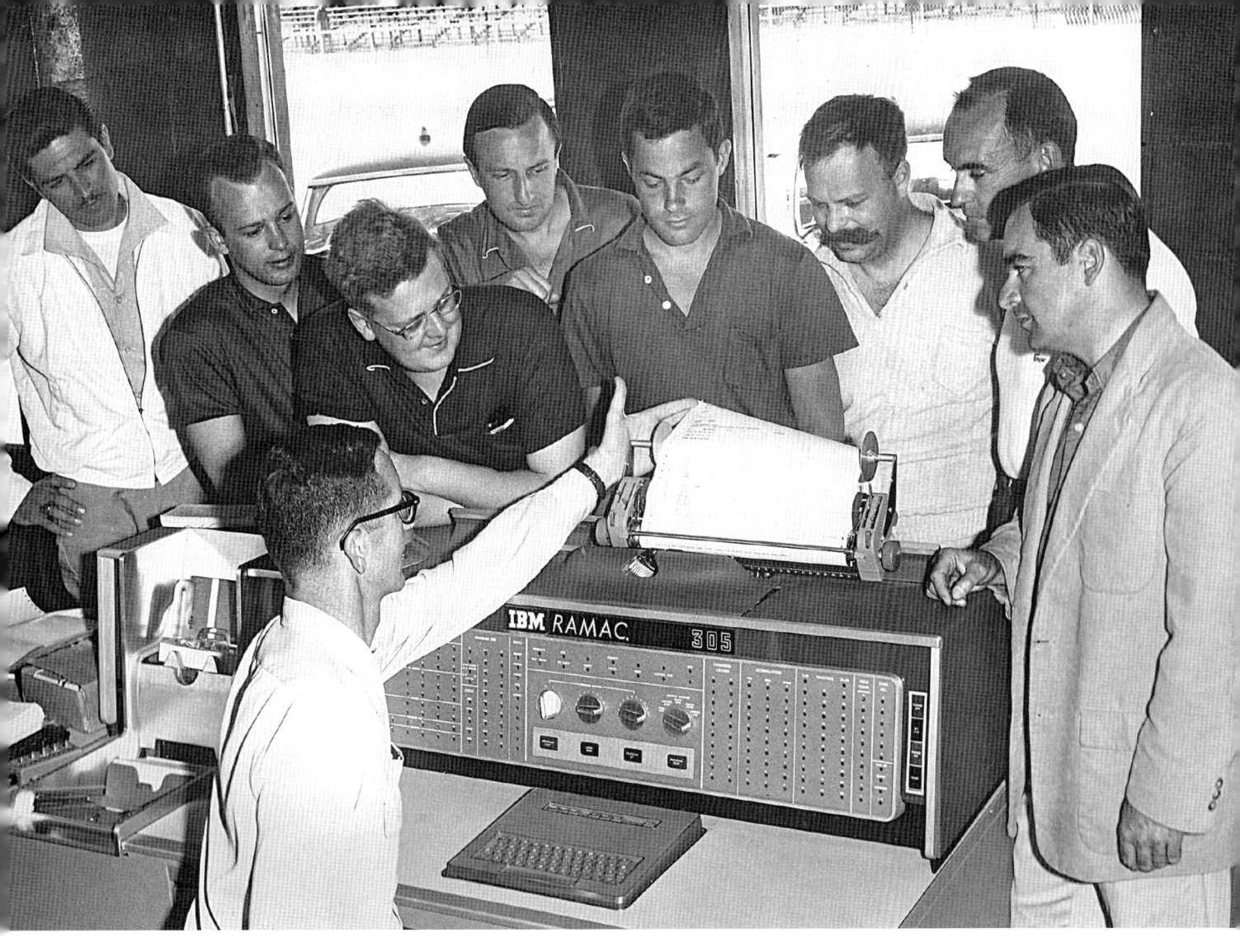

Peter Riley (on the left; wearing glasses, leaning on the counter), and Jack Sears, behind him, check out IBM's new-fangled electric timing for the 12 Hour Sebring race in 1960. Team manager, Geoff Healey (with moustache), looks on. (Jack Sears Archive)

close to Sebring. As Peter Riley recalls: "The Americans were totally fascinated by this typically English gentleman, dressed immaculately in the English style. They were even more impressed at the swimming pool when Jack dived in; as he came up his hands appeared first, outstretched, and he immediately stroked his hair down smoothly as his head broke the surface. He made a great impression on them with this gesture ... they thought they were now watching a true English gentleman.

"Ironically, Jack and I are now in our seventies and just the other month Jack looked at me and said 'I am so glad you have done something about your hair'. I had let my hair grow longer; obviously Jack still has a thing about his hair."

Five cars had been entered for Sebring by BMC USA that year: two MGAs and three Austin-Healey 3000s. Fellow British drivers Colin Escott and veteran MG driver Ted Lund shared an MGA with Phil Stiles and Jack Flaherty, and Jim Parkinson drove the other MGA, also with Phil Stiles as the third driver. In the Austin-Healey camp were Gil Geitner and Lew Spencer, John Colgate Junior and Fred Spross.

As with many long distance races it was a hard slog with the Austin-Healey; Peter Riley remembers one dramatic incident. "The cars actually went well but one of the American cars driven by John Colgate rolled it in the Esses and I came round to find the Healey upside down and all I could see was the driver's arm sticking out. It looked absolutely horrendous but the marshals lifted it up and he got out. I also remember

Maybe Jack Sears didn't win Sebring in 1960 with the Austin-Healey 3000, but he did manage to bag Miss Sebring. (Jack Sears Archive)

turn one and two – not very imaginative names – which were left kinks, not corners. There was just enough room for a Ferrari to pass a Healey but it was tight. However, Sebring, was the nicest airfield circuit I had ever driven on because it had a wide selection of curves and bends. It was great fun for both Jack and I on our first visit to America."

It was not a very successful trip, however, as the car repeatedly suffered from gearbox trouble. Jack and Peter struggled to the end finishing 33rd and last of the finishers, 55 laps behind the winning Porsche RS60 of Hans Herrmann and Jo Bonnier. The sister car of Gil Geitner and Lew Spencer finished 15th overall.

Despite this disappointing result Marcus Chambers then asked if they would like to take the same Austin-Healey 3000 to Le Mans. (Then registered UJB143, it was later sold to David Dixon who re-registered the car DD300, then passed to John Chatham who owned it for forty years. It is probably the most successful Austin-Healey 3000 ever raced.)

The Le Mans attempt in 1960 was also something of a disappointment as the Sears/Riley Austin-Healey 3000 ran its engine bearings.

To give some idea of how factory drives operated back then, the car was works supported with factory mechanics, but Jack and Peter Riley had to get the car out to Le Mans themselves and book their own accommodation. They were staying in a slightly rundown chateau that was more two-star than five-star and the car was towed out on a trailer behind an Austin A105 saloon. Jack, meanwhile, had gone into business with a local Norfolk man called Bill Pledger, who was in haulage and wanted to diversify into the hire

Jack approaching the Esses with the factory Austin-Healey 3000 at the 1960 Le Mans 24 Hour race. (Jack Sears Archive)

The factory Austin-Healey 3000 shared by Jack Sears and Peter Riley at Le Mans in 1960. (Jack Sears Archive)

of motorised caravans. They started out with normal Austin vans and had them converted into motor homes. Called Caracars eight were eventually produced although the switch was then made to Commers as they were slightly bigger. Jack and Cicely drove one of these motor homes to Le Mans and this became the team's base in the paddock. Cicely was roped in to do the catering for the team and the caravan provided an ideal place for the drivers to snatch some sleep.

The race was relatively short and sweet. Clearly, the Austin-Healey 3000 was no match for the 3 litre Ferrari 250GT SWBs, which took fourth, fifth, sixth and seventh places overall, and the car was retired after 89 laps with what was reported as engine trouble. In fact, back at the factory, they found some swarf that had been left between the engine and the oil cooler had circulated, blocking the oil pipe and running the big ends.

These were the only two races Jack Sears drove for BMC that year.

Above: Le Mans 1960: Jack Sears in action with the factory Austin-Healey 3000. (Jack Sears Archive)

The Sears/Riley Austin-Healey, behind the number 17 Testa Rossa of Ricardo Rodriguez, is squeezed in by the 4th place Ferrari 250GT (16) of Fernand Tavano at the 1960 Le Mans 24 Hour race, Jack's first Le Mans. (Jack Sears Archive)

Dabbling in Formula 2 & an introduction to Ferrari

Jack Sears never entertained an ambition to drive single-seater racing cars, but Ken Gregory – who ran the Yeoman-Credit Formula 2 racing team as part of the British Racing Partnership – telephoned him out of the blue to ask if he would like to drive their Formula 2 Cooper (Cooper 51 F2-1-59) at Crystal Palace. "I said, wow; that's an amazing offer but I am under contract to Tommy Sopwith, and though we don't have a race that weekend I feel I must speak to him first. Tommy said that would be fine but to be careful, and so I was invited to Snetterton to do a few laps in the car."

The British Racing Partnership was established in 1958 by Alfred Moss and Ken Gregory with a double purpose. Firstly, it meant they could run Stirling Moss when he was not committed to set contracts, and at the same time have cars available that they could offer to promising young British drivers. In this respect BRP deserves much more credit than has ever been given as it helped to develop the talents of Tony Brooks, Ivor Bueb, Stuart Lewis-Evans, Henry Taylor and Chris Bristow. The following year BRP developed Borgward engines to run in its Formula 2 Coopers, and bought a Grand Prix BRM that Stirling Moss raced in non-championship events.

In 1960 BRP was approached by the Yeoman Credit company, which wanted to sponsor a team of Cooper Climaxes under the Yeoman Credit banner. It was one of these 1960 Coopers that Jack was to drive at Crystal Palace. He says: "The race was on Whitsun Monday and I drove to Crystal Palace on the Saturday only to be met by Tony Robinson, the chief mechanic, who told me he had dreadful news. The engine had caught fire and burned out all the electrics and the car was in no condition to qualify."

At this, Tony and his mechanics dashed back to the workshops with the car to check out the engine, rewire it and then get it back to Crystal Palace by the Monday morning. That day dawned dull and wet and Jack was initially concerned that this was his first race in a Formula 2 car he hardly knew. It was wet but Jack reasoned that he was always quite good in the wet and so should go out, forget it was a single-seater and just drive. Luckily for him he knew the circuit. The club organising the meeting was aware of this and said it would send him out for the minimum three qualifying laps but that he would have to start from the back of the grid. Remembers Jack: "There I was, at the back of the grid in the rain, the flag dropped and off I went only to find some of the cars ahead of me were running quite slowly. I started overtaking cars and continued like that; by the end of the race I was in third place behind Trevor Taylor having his first Formula 2 race for Lotus in a Lotus 18 (372), New Zealander

49

GENTLEMAN JACK

George Lawton's Cooper 45 (F1/12/58), and had equalled Trevor Taylor's fastest lap! Ken Gregory was overjoyed, so much so that he asked if I would do another race, this time at Snetterton."

The Snetterton race – the Vanwall Trophy for Formula 2 cars – took place exactly two months later. Jack was driving the team's other Cooper 51, chassis number F2-24-59 and, as it turned out, problems with the electrics on the car forced him to retire after just three laps. His friend, Mike McKee, won the event in the Jim Russell Racing Drivers' School Cooper 45. "At the end of the race Ken Gregory told me I had been doing okay and would I like to join the team for the rest of the Formula 2 season? I said I would think about it. I reasoned that I was really just an enthusiastic racing driver, happy and lucky to be driving for Tommy Sopwith. I now had a young family; David was five and Suzanne was 4, and a farm to run, so I took a deliberate view about this and turned the offer down. Indeed, those two drives in the Cooper and one drive in Nobby Spero's ex-Dick Seaman pre-war Maserati are the only single-seater drives I have ever had."

The British Grand Prix saloon car race was always a classic but John Coombs realised he could not run Roy Salvadori in his usual 3.8 litre Jaguar as he was racing in the Grand Prix. Meanwhile, aside from this, Colin Chapman of Lotus had expressed to Jaguar competitions manager, Lofty England, an interest in buying a 3.8 Jaguar. Lofty told Colin that Salvadori was unable to drive the Coombs car so why didn't he drive it in the race? Colin thought this was a wonderful idea and, in his usual smooth manner, Lofty England persuaded John Coombs that it would be a good idea if Colin Chapman drove his Jaguar against Jack Sears in the Sopwith car.

"The race started and Colin and I got engaged in the mother and father of all dices. We were passing and re-passing for the whole race and it was absolutely terrific. We kissed each other once or twice; not a bang but we touched a few times. It was funny that after the race neither of us could see any damage to the cars so it must have been the gentlest of touching – unlike what goes on in saloon car racing today. On the last lap we came down Hanger Straight at Silverstone and through Stowe with me in the lead and Colin right behind. Coming out of Club and heading up to the left-hand sweep of Abbey there was a back marker we were about to lap. I started flashing my lights and the

What saloon car racing was all about. Jack Sears, in the Equipe Endeavour Jaguar 3.8, leads Sir Gawaine Baillie (Jaguar) and a hard-charging Colin Chapman in John Coombs' 3.8 litre Jaguar. (Jack Sears Archive)

Colin Chapman, in the John Coombs Jaguar 3.8, chases Jack Sears through Club Corner at Silverstone. (Jack Sears Archive)

Mini beware: Jack Sears and Colin Chapman in their epic duel at Silverstone about to lap an unsuspecting Mini. Note how the crafty Chapman is boxing in Sears behind the Mini. (Jack Sears Archive)

GENTLEMAN JACK

marshal on the outside of Abbey was waving his blue flag at the slower car: it was one of these things I can see in slow motion even now. I was going to get to this bloke right on the apex of Abbey which was taken absolutely flat. He was on the right so I reasoned that as I had flashed my lights he would stay there and I would slip through on the inside but, of course, he didn't. He moved across to take what he thought was the perfect line and I had to take my foot off the accelerator. I lost enough momentum to change down to third and pulled past him heading for Woodcote and the finish but Colin had not lost as much momentum. He drew alongside me which meant he was on the inside for the run into Woodcote and I was out in the cold on his left. Colin won the race; we shook hands afterwards and for many years after we used to recall that as one of our favourite races. I think it is fair to say Colin did, in fact, buy a Jaguar 3.8 for his own personal use!"

To complete the year Peter Berry offered Jack a drive in the RAC Rally with Willy Cave in a 3.8 litre Jaguar. This was an interesting event as it was the first RAC Rally to incorporate loose surface special stages, thanks to an arrangement with the Forestry Commission. Despite the fact that the car was not exactly the best for pounding along rough forest tracks, it was fully supported by Jaguar. Winner of the RAC that year was that great Swede, Eric Carlsson, with Stuart Turner driving one of the two-stroke Saabs. John Sprinzel surprised everyone by taking second place in an Austin-Healey Sprite, and third was Donald Morley in a Healey 3000. However, Jack Sears came a remarkable fourth in the Jaguar; he says: "I often marvelled at what we did do on that event, especially on loose surfaces. However, Willie Cave's navigation was brilliant. We had fog one night and he would act as radar with his head buried in the map and shout out the distances to the next corner. I was driving much faster than I should have been in the conditions but he was so good at warning me by reading the map – no pace notes, remember – that I felt totally confident in him. It was the best overall classification result I ever had in an international rally and, strangely enough, I was fastest overall on the narrow Rest and Be Thankful hill climb in Scotland and won my race at Brands Hatch."

In April 1961, Jaguar cars launched the sensational E-type Jaguar at the Geneva Motor Show at the astounding price of £1500. Even Jaguar realised that the car had potential for racing, and at the Geneva Motor Show had legendary test driver, Norman Dewis, and Jaguar PR man and racing driver, Bob Berry, on hand to give appropriate demonstrations of the car's potential. Both Tommy Sopwith and John Coombs bought E-types with a view to racing them, and the cars made their debut at Oulton Park on April 15 1961, where Roy Salvadori rolled out the pale grey Coombs car – then registered BUY1 but later registered 4WPD – and Graham Hill appeared in Tommy Sopwith's Equipe Endeavour car. Jack Sears was given the new Ferrari 250GT SWB, bought jointly by Tommy Sopwith and Colonel Ronnie Hoare of Maranello Concessionaires: it was the first time Sears had raced a Ferrari.

Salvadori won the race with Hill in third place, but Jack Sears was very satisfied with fourth place in the Ferrari. A few weeks later at Crystal Palace it was Jack's turn to drive an E-type, and he took the Sopwith car to second place in the GT race. However, later that afternoon, he and Michael Parkes were due to run the Equipe Endeavour 3.8 litre Jaguars against their great rival Roy Salvadori driving John Coombs' 3.8. John Coombs was one of the smartest team owners in the business and, prior to the race, told Salvadori he believed the Equipe Endeavour game plan was for Michael Parkes

First race in a Ferrari. Jack Sears takes the Tommy Sopwith/ Ronnie Hoare 250GT SWB through Old Hall at Oulton Park. (Jack Sears Archive)

Crystal Palace and the Equipe Endeavour Jaguar E-type, one of the most successful of the period. (Jack Sears Archive)

Touring car racing in the 1960s tended to be close. Here, Sears and Roy Salvadori demonstrate that at Brands Hatch. (Jack Sears Archive)

to go out for the win and Jack Sears was to keep an eye on Roy Salvadori, to try and help Parkes get away.

Roy Salvadori was not going to have this and went into the race knowing he was going to have to tame Jack Sears. As he admitted later, he was so juiced up about it all he made a bad start and the two Endeavour cars took the lead. During the second lap Roy was right on Jack Sears' tail and pressing hard. At Tower Corner he decided to take the inside line and ploughed across the grass and the kerb in an effort to force his way through. Jack Sears may have been a gentleman but he was a very determined one and held his line, simply refusing to move over. Needless to say, the two 3.8 Jaguars came together, and Sears was bounced across the road and into the railway sleepers that marked the edge of the track, breaking the back axle. Meanwhile, Roy Salvadori was off after Michael Parkes. Two laps later Parkes had a wheel come off his Jaguar and Salvadori stroked his way home for a win. In his biography Roy Salvadori says:

"After the race John [Coombs] seemed to be disowning me and was consoling Tommy Sopwith, but I did get a thumbs up from John when Tommy was looking the other way."

Jack was again enlisted to the BMC team to race at the 1962 12 Hours of Sebring event, and once more the team was based at the Avon Park motel. There was a little lake beside the motel and the owner offered Jack his boat to go water ski-ing. John Whitmore had never water-skied before, but Jack had skied so had no problem getting up on the skis quite quickly. John had to learn how to do it but anyone who knows him will tell you that he is a great enthusiast who will try anything: he learned to water ski on that visit.

This was the year that BMC USA decided to run a raft of Austin-Healey Sebring Sprites in the 3 hour race for small capacity sports cars the day before the main event, enlisting a team of big names to drive them. Stirling Moss, Pedro Rodriguez and Innes Ireland were all given Sprites, with a fourth car going to film star and racing enthusiast,

In the 1962 Sebring 12 Hour race, Jack Sears and Andrew Hedges paired up in a factory MkII MGA, finishing 4th in their Class. (Jack Sears Archive)

Steve McQueen. "The name Steve McQueen really meant nothing to us." says Jack. "However, he was famous in America as the star of an American western TV series called *Wanted Dead or Alive*. Stirling did not stay with us but Steve did and so was part of our group. All of us were captivated by this Steve McQueen who was a very charismatic guy, and after an hour or two in his company I could see why he was a television star. Wherever he went people were queuing up for his autograph. I must say I never saw one of his TV programmes but later on I always enjoyed his films, particularly *Bullit*."

At that Sebring event Jack was racing one of the factory MGA Coupés with Andrew Hedges. BMC USA wanted to promote the Coupé very seriously in the USA as the earlier MGA Twin-Cams had proved unreliable and were dropped by BMC. Jack and Andrew did well to finish 16th overall in the race against the factory Ferraris and the like.

Back in England Equipe Endeavour entered Michael Parkes and Jack Sears for the saloon car race at Snetterton just before the British Grand Prix. During practice Sears was following Parkes into Coram Curve when the left-hand back wheel came off Parkes' car and the Jaguar hit the banking hard. Sears immediately dashed into the pits to tell Tommy Sopwith what had happened. As it turned out, a half shaft had sheared and Sopwith told Jack he was withdrawing his car from the race until they had checked over the damage to the Parkes car. Sopwith then decided to change the half shafts on the Jaguars more regularly.

This created a problem, however, because one week later was the Blue Riband touring car race of the British year, the one that supported the British Grand Prix at Aintree. Tommy Sopwith realised that the Parkes car would not be repaired in time so telephoned another 3.8 Jaguar entrant, Peter Berry, and asked if he could hire one of his 3.8s for Jack to drive. He explained that the car would be taken back to the Equipe Endeavour workshops and all its bits would be transferred to the Berry car. (It's worth mentioning here that one of the great advantages Tommy Sopwith had over the other entrants was access to Michael Parkes, a gifted senior engineer with the Rootes Group, who later moved to Scuderia Ferrari as an engineer and driver.)

As a result, Equipe Endeavour ran two Jaguars, for Michael Parkes and Jack Sears, with Sears in the dark green Peter Berry car. Lined up against them was the mercurial Australian driver, Bob Jane, in John Coombs' pale grey 3.8 Jaguar. Jane was at the height of his saloon car racing career and won the Australian Touring Car Championship that season. He was a spectacular driver to watch, clearly out to show the 'Poms' how to race saloon cars. This made Jack Sears all the more determined to beat him out on the track. "Michael and I introduced ourselves to Bob in the paddock. He wasn't that tall but had a self-assurance which indicated to me that he was letting me know he was Australian saloon car champion and we were quite lucky to be in his presence. Don't misunderstand me; he was a very nice guy, but he was certainly aware of his status."

To anyone at Aintree that day, the saloon car event was one of the most exciting and memorable races of all time. There seemed little doubt that the three Jaguars would dominate, which is what happened, the rest of the field forgotten about. At the start Bob Jane leaped into the lead with Michael Parkes tucking in behind him and Jack Sears in third place. Initially, the three Jaguars were virtually tied together, then began chopping and changing. After a few laps Jack Sears was in the lead with Bob Jane behind him and Parkes on Jane's back bumper. At the end of the back straight leading into Melling Crossing Bob Jane's Jaguar was suddenly at right angles to the other two Jaguars and spun, wreathed in tyre smoke. Jane fought his way back into the lead and then, once more at Melling Crossing, was slightly off-line for this high speed left-hand swerve. He shot across the road onto the grass; Michael Parkes was so close that he, too, drove onto the grass to avoid hitting Jane. Jack Sears was able to overtake them both and go into the lead. Jane and Parkes continued in the race with Parkes beginning to catch Jack in the closing laps. As Jack recalls: "I came across the start and finish line in the lead with only a few laps to go. Strangely, I always did well at Aintree, no matter what I drove. It was a funny circuit and not everybody's cup of tea but I enjoyed it. I thought to myself, I can win this race; why shouldn't I win, Michael Parkes has been beating me all year so why can't I have a win? At this point Bob Jane was now second and Michael was third. I was lapping quicker than Bob Jane and was pulling away from him so thought that if I kept up this pressure he had had it. I then started to think, come on, Michael, you've got to get past this Australian and Michael duly did. Then Michael started to close up on me. He got fairly close and I thought I had better let him get by so I gestured for him to do so but he just waved and stayed behind me and let me win the race."

A learned London judge once remarked: "If you listen to two drivers describing a road accident you will never believe in history." As if to prove this theory, here is Bob Jane's recent recollections of the same race and his fellow drivers.

"I had come over to Jaguar to pick up my new E-type, and Lofty England offered me a drive in the coming Grand Prix event some months later, which I accepted. I then spent some time with Bruce McLaren, Jack Brabham and John Cooper at the Formula 1 races at Reims, and Rouen. On my return to England I had to go to Coombs' Jaguar dealership to inspect the car that I was to race. As you probably know, in those days Graham Hill and Roy Salvadori were driving for John Coombs, and Jack Sears and Michael Parkes were driving for Equipe Endeavour. Due to the fact I didn't know

Aintree Incident 1: Jack Sears, in the Peter Berry Jaguar 3.8 loaned to Equipe Endeavour, leads team-mate, Michael Parkes, and Australian, Bob Jane, in the John Coombs 3.8. (Jack Sears Archive)

Aintree Incident 2: Jack Sears leads but, behind him, Bob Jane is nudged sideways by Michael Parkes. (Jack Sears Archive)

Dabbling in Formula 2 & an introduction to Ferrari

Aintree Incident 3: Bob Jane takes the wrong line through Melling Crossing after another nudge by Michael Parkes. (Jack Sears Archive)

Aintree Incident 4: Bob Jane takes to the grass in the Coombs 3.8 litre Jaguar. (Jack Sears Archive)

Graham Hill that well, I wasn't offered Graham's car but was given Roy Salvadori's, which had recently been driven into a lake at a race meeting earlier that year. Frankly, it was not a very impressive car but I worked with the mechanic allocated to me and spent some time on the ratios and suspension height. On the Thursday of first practice I had pole position. This situation sent a message to the Jaguar factory which started paying attention and wanted to help me. I retained pole position on Friday and Saturday, which was of great interest to Bruce McLaren and Jack Brabham as most of the Formula One drivers at that time really enjoyed the saloon car racing."

However, Jane was not happy about the engine in his car: "The Salvadori car had head gasket problems so on the Saturday the Jaguar people promised to fix it for me. As we had had some problems back in Australia with our head gaskets I gave them the solution; however they chose to ignore my advice.

"During the race I was leading and, to my recollection, Michael Parkes stabbed me up the bum and spun me off on one of the corners. I caught both Jaguars of Michael and Jack and I recall being hit again and went off at Melling Crossing. By this time my head gasket had blown. I later found out that the race had been so exciting that Jim Clark and Bruce McLaren, watching from the BP tanker in the paddock, fell off!

"After the race Michael Parkes came up to me and in his very British and polite manner said 'I say, old chap, we don't drive like that here.' My reply was 'stiff shit old chap, that's how I drive, anyway.'

"In one way it was a great race and in another it was a disappointment because I didn't finish. Jaguar was shocked to see its worst Jaguar, Roy Salvadori's, the fastest car in the race which had held pole for three whole days, and had some difficulty comprehending how this Rambo from Australia could do this."

Jack Sears does not exactly agree with Bob's description of the race: "In my opinion his recollection of driving between

For the 1962 Tour de France Rally, Jack took up an offer to drive Frenchman, Claude Lego's, 3.8 litre Jaguar, but this ended in a huge accident at Clermont Ferrand. (Jack Sears Archive)

Dabbling in Formula 2 & an introduction to Ferrari

Michael and myself and knocking our door handles off, his, too, in order to regain the lead, is a figment of his imagination as both our cars finished complete with handles!"

One day, out of the blue came an invitation from Frenchman, Claude Lego, for Jack Sears to co-drive his red, left-hand drive Jaguar 3.8 in the 1962 Tour de France rally. The arrangement they agreed was that Jack would do all the races and Claude would do all the hill climbs. Lego also asked Jack if he could use his influence to get Equipe Endeavour to prepare his car to the same specification as the racing Jaguars. Sir Gawaine Baillie entered his own 3.8 litre Jaguar with racing driver Peter Jopp as his co-driver, but the threat to them both was the charming and successful French rally and racing driver Bernard Consten, who was out to win his third in a row Tour de France for Jaguar.

Bernard was clearly a favoured customer of Jaguar Competitions Department, but was horrified to arrive at scrutineering and find the Baillie and Lego cars fitted with larger, 2 inch SU carburettors, just homologated to replace the standard 1½ inch versions. Consten immediately telephoned Lofty England to complain that the factory had prepared his car but that these two privately-entered cars had turned up with bigger carburettors.

"It was an international incident ..." says Jack "... a question of whether our two cars were eligible as Bernard was challenging their eligibility. All the paperwork was correct, there had been an homologation paper for the bigger carburettors and this had been produced. The problem for Consten was that he clearly should have had them on his car and was mighty put out about it."

Bernard Consten, still a great enthusiast with a fine collection of cars, including one of his 3.8 litre Jaguars, lives in retirement near Grasse in the South of France. He won the Touring Class in the Tour de France Rally no fewer than five times; once with an Alfa Romeo and the rest with Jaguars. He also raced at Le Mans and Sebring and was the man to beat in this particular event. He still chuckles when he recalls from his point of view what happened in 1962. "What you must understand is that Claude Lego's wife, Denise, had this great ambition for Claude to beat me on an event. I knew there was no way he was going to do it, and I think that is why he thought about inviting Jack Sears to drive in the racing events."

Consten remembered that, earlier in 1962, Monsieur Delacroix, the Paris Jaguar importer, received a telephone call from a member of Lofty England's staff saying that they were in the middle of preparing Consten's car and did he want the third fuel tank added? Consten asked why a third fuel tank was now available and was told that in the 1961 Tour de France he had finished the Le Mans race with only two or three litres of fuel left in the tank, so the third tank was a precaution. After confirming that the cars would have no more power, and that fuel consumption remained the same, Consten decided not to have the third tank fitted. Despite the fact that Jaguar was preparing the engine for Consten's car, the preparation was actually done in John Coombs' workshops in Guildford.

However, when Consten arrived at Rouen for scrutineering he was in for a surprise. " Obviously, I knew all the scrutineers and when I brought my car they all asked me why I had the smaller 1½ inch SU carburettors when the two English Jaguars had 2 inch SUs. Well, I was furious and thought the English were trying to put one over on me. I telephoned Lofty England to find that the 2 inch carburettors had been homologated but had not been fitted to my car. Lofty told me not to worry; they might gain in outright speed but not in acceleration.

"Well, at the Rouen race that started the event both Jack Sears and Peter Jopp shot off ahead and I didn't see them again until on the last lap when I saw them in my mirrors coming up to lap me!"

The same thing happened at Le Mans, only this time it was a two hour race. "Even though it was a 14km lap I saw the two Jaguars catching me. I was absolutely green with anger so drove the Jaguar flat-out and waited for it to break but it was so solid it just wouldn't break, though clearly at this rate I was not going to win my third Tour in a row."

As it transpired, fate took a hand when the rally moved on to the Clermont-Ferrand circuit and the picture changed drastically. Once more Jack Sears was out in the lead in his race and came up to lap Citroën DS factory driver, Andre Marang. Marang did not see the Jaguar about to pounce and moved over to take his normal line; the cars touched and Sears went off the road at high speed, hitting the banking hard and overturning. As it had been a Le Mans start Sears did not have time to fix his seat belts and the impact threw him through the car and out the back window. Jack was taken off to hospital with four cracked spinal vertebrae, his rally over. He never understood how Marang had not seen him as he had his headlights on and was flashing them: even the marshals were waving a blue flag at Marang.

As for Bernard Consten: "I came down the hill to the Gravenoir Corner and saw Jack Sears' red Jaguar on its roof with Marang's Citroën beside it. I could see both drivers and they seemed to be arguing; all of a sudden, I noticed that the photographers around the track were taking my picture, which I thought strange because as far as I was aware we were not in second place. However, when I finished the race my co-driver, Jack Revel, rushed over to me and said it was wonderful and told me that the Gawaine Baillie Jaguar had also crashed at the next bend. I had not even noticed the black tyre marks where Baillie appeared to have missed his braking point, but knew then that I could be on my way to winning my third Tour de France."

The result of Jack Sears' accident at Clermont-Ferrand during the 1963 Tour de France rally, when he was forced off the road by a Citroën. (Jack Sears Archive)

Looking back on the accident Jack Sears explains the seat belts problem: "I had planned to get into the car and put the seat belts on, but in the heat of the moment I left them off. Unbelieveably, Gawaine Baillie was lying second behind me and he, too, went off, both of us ending up side-by-side in the same hospital in Clermont Ferrand, comforting each other. The bottom line was Bernard Consten went on to win the Tour de France with his small carburettors, so must have thought the good Lord was smiling on him. He and I have joked about it many times since, though I still don't understand how he ended up with the little carburettors."

The accident was quite a blow for Jack, who was in a plaster cast for several months after that. He remembers the surgeon sticking pins in his feet to test his reactions; luckily, his spinal cord was not affected. The surgeon left a hole in the cast around his stomach and Jack asked why: "Ah monsieur, c'est pour le vin rouge et le fromage."

On his return to Norfolk Jack spoke to his doctor, who advised that he should contact the well-known local orthopaedic surgeon, Ken McKee, and ask his advice. McKee took one look at the elaborate plaster cast and immediately attacked it with his circular saw, replacing it with a plastic jacket similar to a woman's corset that Jack could take off to shower.

To this day Jack Sears has not had any trouble arising from those serious injuries, although the accident ended his racing for 1962. He also left Tommy Sopwith and Equipe Endeavour: "I had three wonderful years with Tommy and it was great fun to be team mate to Michael Parkes, even though he was always quicker than me." (As it turned out

1963 was to become a special year for Jack Sears, in which he confirmed that he was probably Britain's finest saloon car driver. He also raced for Maranello Concessionaires with not only the Ferrari GTO but also the 330LMB at Le Mans.)

It was around this time, the end of 1962, that Jack Sears met Enzo Ferrari for the first time. Because of the close friendship between Tommy Sopwith and Colonel Ronnie Hoare of Maranello Concessionaires, Hoare was well aware of the racing and engineering talent of Michael Parkes. It was Hoare who started pushing Enzo Ferrari to consider hiring Parkes, not only as a development engineer but also a sports car driver for Scuderia Ferrari. At the time, Parkes was a development engineer with the Rootes Group and had a lot to do with development of the Hillman Imp.

Ronnie Hoare arranged to bring Michael Parkes to Maranello to meet Enzo Ferrari and discuss his plans (for 1953, but asked if both Tommy Sopwith – who had been running Parkes in his team – and Michael's team mate, Jack Sears, could come with them, which was agreed.

As Parkes, Sopwith and Sears did not speak Italian they were taken round the factory by Ing Manicardi, and in particular shown round the racing department where Michael Parkes would be working. Remembers Jack: "I was a fairly silent witness to all of this and just felt lucky to be going along for the ride, but I remember that the entire proceedings were conducted in Italian and if Michael needed a translation Manicardi was there, as was Ronnie Hoare who spoke fluent Italian. Tommy Sopwith and I just sat there fascinated, watching this little scenario unfold.

"We were then taken over to the Cavallino restaurant where Enzo Ferrari had the private room in the back. It is surprising that recently, when visiting Maranello as Chairman of the Ferrari Owners' Club in Britain, I discovered that the back room is still kept private, used by Luca di Montezemolo, current President of Ferrari."

Why not visit Veloce on the web? – www.velocebooks.com
New book news • Special offers • Details of all books in print • Gift vouchers

THE CORTINA DAYS

5

The year 1963 came in like a lion with Britain's Great Freeze as Siberian weather hit the British Isles with a vengeance. It lasted for two and a half months and the temperature never rose above freezing; the coldest winter of the 20th century, the frost sinking eighteen inches into the soil. Luckily for Jack Sears the farmer, all his sugar beet had already been lifted, though there was little else he could do on the farm.

In the middle of January, Jack had a phone call from Jeff Uren, one of his great rivals in British saloon car racing,

Willment team manager and Jack's ex-competitor in saloon car racing, Jeff Uren, right. (Jack Sears Archive)

Jack with the Lotus Cortina. (Courtesy Ford Motor Co)

who had been very successful with a Ford Zephyr. Jeff announced he had been appointed team manager to the newly-formed John Willment Racing Team, which had a few Ford dealerships in the south and now wanted to form a racing team to promote these. Uren went on to explain that they were arranging to have a full-house Holman and Moody NASCAR Ford Galaxie built and sent over to England for the British Saloon Car Championship, and he wanted Jack to race it.

Jack's first question was to ask whether a NASCAR Galaxie was eligible for the British Championship, and Jeff Uren confirmed that indeed it was. Jack remarked that the car would surely never handle or stop on British circuits, and reminded Jeff of the time that Dan Gurney had brought a Chevrolet Impala to Silverstone to race. [Dan Gurney recalls: "Man, that car looked like an aircraft carrier amongst those European cars."] Though the Impala was quick the problem was that the wheels could not take the strain and Gurney was sidelined when he lost a wheel.

Jeff was insistent that everything would be sorted out. Jack asked if, perhaps, he could have a trial drive in it but was told this was impossible as the car had not even been built! Jeff added that though the car would probably not reach Britain until the spring, he needed a decision from Jack; additionally, until the Galaxie arrived he would have to race a Ford Cortina GT. Jack thought that Jeff Uren was pulling his leg as the Ford Cortina – a family saloon launched in the autumn of 1962 – did not appear to be a race car. "It's not generally known, and keep it under your hat" said Jeff, "but there is going to be a GT version and it will appear in March. It will be a hotted up version of the cooking Cortina with a 1500cc engine rather than a 1200 unit, and we would like you to drive that until the Galaxie comes."

After the phone call Jack discussed the proposition with his wife, Cicely. Although being asked to sign up to race two cars that he could not even drive, he decided to take a chance and signed with Jeff Uren to race for the Willment team.

The plan was to race the Cortina GT straight out of the box on March 30 in the Lombank Trophy at Snetterton, but the car was unable to start because the homologation papers had not come through in time. Luckily, there was the spring meeting at Oulton Park the following weekend (April 6) with a round in the British Saloon Car Championship; as Jeff Uren had now collected the homologation papers the Ford Cortina GT made its world debut at this meeting.

However, things did not start well in first practice. "Off I went in my Cortina GT and the bloody thing just would not go at all. It was hesitating, wouldn't rev properly, and was an absolute disaster. I kept coming into the pits and they checked everything, distributor, coil, everything and all of a sudden practice was over. I had done my requisite three laps but, because of the problems, was at the back of the grid, the car was so bog slow. I didn't sleep very well and thought it was really a joke. However, the next day we lined up for the race and did a warm-up lap and, all of a sudden, the car went like a dream; it felt quick and it handled and in just one lap I made friends with this car. I was right at the back of the grid and at the end of the warm-up lap I jumped out of the car and had a word with some of the Mini drivers at the back of the grid with me. I explained the car was running like a dream and that I would probably out-accelerate them so would they try and not close the gap and let me go through because we were not in the same capacity Class."

The race started and the white Willment Cortina GT suddenly leaped from the back of the grid and began to plough its way through the gaggle of Minis to catch up on the 1.5 litre cars. The main contenders in this Class were Peter Harper in his Sunbeam Rapier and Allan Hutchison with his Riley 1.5. Coming out of the hairpin Jack caught up with Harper. "I took the outside line and, as we reached the brow of the hill before the plunge down to Knickerbrook, I was alongside Peter. He looked across at me and I looked across at him and gave him the thumbs up. Now I had to catch Alan Hutchison as he was the man I had to beat; like a red rag to a bull, I was determined to get ahead of that Riley 1.5."

Jack did catch and pass Hutchison but then Hutchison re-passed and the pair kept passing and re-passing each other for the last half of the race. On the last lap Hutchison was in the lead until Lodge Corner when Sears did the ultimate late braking manoeuvre and squeezed through on the inside of the Riley, managing to hold on to the lead by half a car's length. So the Cortina GT won first time out: "I remember coming up to the line and, out of the corner of my eye, seeing Colin Chapman rush forward and throw his cap into the air. It gave a huge boost to my confidence as the only cars ahead of me were the Jaguars of Graham Hill and Roy Salvadori."

With the Cortina GT Sears went on to win his Class in every single race that year, the only serious opposition in the Class coming from Jimmy Blumer driving the rival Alan Mann Cortina GT.

Meanwhile, in the States, Holman and Moody were working on the new Ford Galaxie for Willment, which looked likely to make its debut at the *Daily Express* Trophy meeting at Silverstone in May, a big event with practice on both Thursday and Friday and the race on Saturday. When Jack arrived on Thursday morning the Galaxie was there but its Firestone racing tyres had not arrived from the States. Jeff Uren apologised and explained it was not his fault as Firestone had not sent the tyres in time. However, Jack took the car, on cooking tyres, to one of the inner runways and ran it up and down to see what it felt like. Then came official saloon car practice and Jack persuaded Jeff Uren that he should go out in the car with the road tyres pumped up to 50 or 60lb to get the feel of the car and check out the brakes. Uren agreed but told Jack to be careful. He did a couple of laps and then decided to try full power through Chapel and on to the Hanger Straight. Suddenly, there was a bang and the rear tyre blew. Jack rolled the car onto the grass on the inside and got out. Graham Hill went past, giving him two fingers; Roy Salvadori waved; Gawaine Baillie waved, as an embarrassed Jack stood and watched.

On the Friday morning the Firestone racing tyres arrived and Jack attended the second practice session. Without trying hard he took pole position from the Jaguars by about one second, but hadn't had time to try a standing start, so once more went to one of the inner runways to try this. On his second standing start the clutch started slipping, and Jack realised he had really been stupid, admitting to Jeff Uren what he had done. Uren said it was okay as they had a spare clutch. Uren phoned John Holman at Holman and Moody in the States and explained what had happened. Holman told him that first gear on a NASCAR Galaxie was very high as they did rolling starts, but that he should tell Jack not to dump the clutch at the start because the clutch would not tolerate it.

On race day Jeff Uren gave Jack his orders: no fancy starts, let the clutch in gently and when the clutch is right back give it a boot-full. "I must say I made a very leisurely start, I mean, it was really leisurely, and into the first corners the three Jaguars were leading with Graham Hill followed by Roy Salvadori and Gawaine Baillie.

"In that first race I had drum brakes with metal to metal linings so they didn't fade and were actually quite good, better than you would believe. I found that the Jaguars were not outbraking me so when we left Chapel Corner and came on to Hanger Straight I felt, gosh, this thing is really flying, I think I can pass them. To my surprise I passed all three Jaguars in the one manoeuvre. I had no time for waving or anything like that; I had my head down concentrating but now was the moment of truth as I hit my braking point

The first outing of the Willment Ford Galaxie at Silverstone. Jack Sears lines up alongside the Jaguars. (Jack Sears Archive)

Galaxie debut. Jack takes it easy off the line at Silverstone in the John Willment Ford Galaxie with Graham Hill and Roy Salvadori (both John Coombs Jaguar 3.8s) alongside. (Courtesy Nick Loudon)

The crucial moment when Jack Sears swept past the three Jaguar 3.8s of Graham Hill, Roy Salvadori and Gawaine Baillie at the end of the Hanger Straight at Silverstone, so marking the cessation of Jaguar domination in British saloon car racing. (Jack Sears Archive)

Jack Sears leads the Jaguars at the end of the first lap of the saloon car race supporting the British Grand Prix at Silverstone. This was the Galaxie's first win. (Jack Sears Archive)

for Stowe. To my surprise they didn't come past me but just followed me. I put my foot down on the exit from the fast uphill left-hander at Abbey and tthe Galaxie just pulled away from the Jaguars. By the end of the second lap I had a comfortable lead though was still worried about the clutch, so left the Galaxie in fourth gear for the rest of the race; I never changed gear again. Tommy Sopwith and Michael Parkes were standing on the inside of Becketts giving me the thumbs up sign, and I even had time to give them and some of my photographer friends a wave."

So now the Galaxie won first time out and Jack Sears felt like he was walking on air. Two weeks later at Aintree he won again but then came the saloon car race at Crystal Palace, a circuit less suited to the big and ungainly-looking Galaxie. Everyone generally agreed that the more nimble Jaguars would have a great advantage, but this was not to be as Sears, in the Galaxie, won again. Indeed, the Galaxie was never beaten that season and it marked the end of Jaguar domination in British saloon car racing. To add to Jaguar's problems Ford homologated front disc brakes on the Galaxie but left it with drums at the rear. To this day Jack has that same Galaxie in his garage at the farm, still with its disc brakes at the front and drum brakes at the rear.

Following the *Express* Trophy win Colonel Ronnie Hoare of Maranello Concessionaires telephoned Jack and invited him to race the Maranello Ferrri 330LMB at Le Mans, with Mike Salmon as his co-driver. Not only did Jack feel honoured to be asked but was also very happy to have Mike as his co-driver, as traditionally Le Mans needs two fast but reliable drivers who can drive with a blend of common sense and sensitivity.

Only four Ferrari 330LMBs were built and three of them competed at Le Mans that year: the Maranello car was Chassis 4725GT, the North American Racing Team car was chassis 4453SA driven by Dan Gurney and Jim Hall, and the Ferrari France entry driven by Jean Guichet and Pierre Noblet

The Willment Galaxie out-performs the Lotus Cortinas at Crystal Palace. (Jack Sears Archive)

BRDC secretary, John Eason Gibson, was on hand to present Jack with the trophy for winning the Saloon Car race in the Ford Galaxie at the 1963 British Grand Prix meeting. (Jack Sears Archive)

In 1963, Jack, with Michael Salmon, finished a creditable 5th overall at Le Mans, winning the over 3 litre GT Class with the Maranello Concessionaires Ferrari 330LMB. Here, Salmon leads the Masten Gregory/David Piper 250GTO with its 330LMB body. (Jack Sears Archive)

was chassis 4381SA. The Maranello car was unique in that it was the only 330LMB built with right-hand drive specifically for Ronnie Hoare. It was road registered 499FX, and ran only twice under the Maranello Concessionaires banner; at Le Mans and the Guards Trophy at Brands Hatch on August 3 when Lorenzo Bandini was the driver. It was sold later that year to a French enthusiast.

A certain amount of confusion surrounds the 330LMB and the 330GTO designations; essentially, 330 referred to the individual cylinder capacity in cubic centimetres of the V12 engine – 3960cc. The 4 litre engine was used for the first time in 250 GTO 3673SA, which Michael Parkes and Willy Mairesse raced to second place overall at the Nürburgring in 1962. Two other 4 litre cars were built with 250 GTO body styling (3765LM and 4561SA). Then came the run of four 'proper' 330LMBs.

To make the confusion even more complex one 3 litre 250GTO was fitted with a 330LMB body (chassis 4713GT), in which, as a passenger, I experienced a number of exciting fast laps of the Modena racing circuit with Michael Parkes driving.

As usual Ferrari people were up to their eyes preparing cars for Le Mans, so Ronnie Hoare flew out to Modena himself to ensure his car was ready for the race. He picked up his 330LMB from Maranello with Italian trade plates and drove the car straight to Le Mans, where it then had its pre-delivery inspection!

Having driven both the 3 litre GTO and the 4 litre 330LMB, Jack was asked by Charles Harbord of Cars for the Connoisseur how he compared the two. "Although the LMB was 4 litres compared to the GTO, it was no more powerful except, perhaps, for an improvement in mid-range torque.

Gentleman Jack

Top speed on the Mulsanne Straight of 175mph was identical in both cases," was his response.

The Sears/Salmon 330LM was one of the heaviest cars in the race, with heavier windows for road use and partly steel-bodied. The car ran with six double-choke carburettors but was later converted to three four-choke carburettors. During the race despite a water leak and clutch trouble, it still finished fifth overall.

Meanwhile, Jeff Uren had organised a test day for other potential drivers, one of whom was a South African called Bob Olthoff who had successfully raced a variety of cars. Olthoff came to Britain with fellow South African, Tony Maggs, racing Austin-Healeys and then a Brabham single-seater. At that same 1963 Le Mans race Olthoff had been paired with Sir John Whitmore in a factory Austin-Healey Sprite. In the fog he misjudged the notorious White House Corner and crashed heavily, suffering a broken collar bone. However, as he had quickly recovered from this Olthoff durly arrived at Silverstone for his test drive, with Jack Sears also present to provide a standard time. As it turned out, Olthoff was the quickest driver after Sears, and got the drive with the team.

At Mallory Park in July, Ronnie Hoare again approached Jack, this time about driving the team's Ferrari GTO (4399GT). Mallory was not the best circuit for a GTO as it was tight, and the GTO was at its best on fast, sweeping bends. Graham Hill was in the John Coombs lightweight Jaguar E-type as he preferred this to the Coombs Ferrari GTO. Jack says: "I got a good start and led the race with Graham right on my tail. Finally, on one of the later laps we came up to the hairpin with me in the middle of the road. I was braking hard for the hairpin and cunning old Graham slipped through on the inside, blocking me off. He was now taking the tightest line round the corner and I was having to take the outside line, so he won the race with me right on his tail."

Jack had a chance to race another GTO when John Coombs offered him his white GTO (3729GT) for the Guards Trophy Race at Brands Hatch, where he was up against Graham Hill in Maranello's Ferrari GTO (4399GT). As this race included prototypes, the GTOs were not in contention for an

Lorenzo Bandini in the Maranello Concessionaires 330LMB Ferrari about to be overtaken by Jack Sears in the John Coombs Ferrari 250GTO, during the Guards Trophy race at Brands Hatch. (Jack Sears Archive)

Four happy Cortina GT drivers after finishing first and second in the Marlboro 12 Hour Saloon Car race in the United States. Left to right: Bob Olthof, Jimmy Blumer, Jack Sears, and Henry Taylor. (Jack Sears Archive)

outright win, and the winner, in fact, was Roger Penske in his Cooper-Zerex special. In the GT Class Graham Hill was in the lead, holding fifth place ahead of Jack Sears, but had to retire with brake trouble. Jack was having a tough race in sixth place, challenging Lorenzo Bandini's 330LMB (4725GT). Bandini slid the LMB on the downhill section from Graham Hill Bend, letting Jack through to fifth overall and first place in the GT Class.

An amusing incident occurred in practice for that race. Bandini was driving the same 330LMB that Jack had raced at Le Mans, but Ronnie Hoare was not particularly happy with Bandini's lap times and quietly asked Jack if he would mind taking out the LMB and doing a few laps if he arranged it with the Clerk of the Course. "The 4 litre 330LMB had only done one race – Le Mans – where Michael Salmon and I had finished fifth overall. It came back to England and was refettled for the Guards Trophy race. I had been asked by John Coombs to drive his regular GTO, and knew the 330LMB didn't handle as well as a GTO: it had a four speed gearbox and four litres and the GTO had a five speed gearbox and three litres.

"When Ronnie asked me to have a few laps in the 330LMB I was able to confirm that the 330LMB did not handle as well as the GTO round the Brands Hatch GP circuit, and

71

First time out: Jack Sears and Peter Arundell debuted the Lotus-Cortina at the 1963 Gold Cup race at Oulton Park. Jack was third overall and won the Class. (Jack Sears Archive)

that a GTO would beat Bandini anyhow." What Sears did not mention was that his lap time in the 330LMB was actually quicker than Bandini's had been!

In August it was back to the USA once more for the Marlboro 12 Hour race, the Alan Mann Cortina GT and the Willment Cortina GT sent with the express purpose of winning as Volvo was reaping a lot of publicity from a string of victories in American saloon car racing. Marlboro was a small circuit like many of the English circuits, and ideally suited the Cortina GT. Three Holman and Moody Ford Falcons were entered, along with a number of big-engined American saloons; however, they were in for a surprise as Jack Sears put the little Cortina GT on pole position in the first practice session. The Americans were stunned. John Holman said to Jeff Uren: "Jeff, can you put Jack's backside into one of those Falcons and let him go round and tell us a few things about the car?"

Uren agreed and John Holman approached Jack with the remark: "I don't know how you are keeping up that pace in that little old car of yours. Will you take the Falcon out and see what you think?" Needless to say, Jack was only too keen to try one and off he went.

"It took me two or three laps to get used to the left-hand drive but it felt just like the Galaxie so I started to put the heat on and in ten laps found myself faster than all six of John Holman's drivers. The drivers were hopping mad and asking who this f*****g Englishman was; to be fair to them I think they did finally get pole position in the later practice session."

Jack's race was not to be as happy, however, as in the opening laps the throttle linkage simply came apart and he had to pit. The problem fixed Jack set off again, now last in the field with eleven hours and fifty minutes to go. Jack took the view that the only thing to do was to treat the event like a sprint race in England: keep the pressure on and hope that co-driver, Bob Olthoff, would also keep on charging. Sears and Olthoff had two advantages over the bigger American cars; they didn't use tyres as quickly as the Falcons did, and the Falcons were also chewing up disc brake pads. The pair literally drove in a red mist and, from being last in the race after the first two laps, stormed home the winners ahead of Henry Taylor and Jimmy Blumer driving the Alan Mann-entered Cortina GT.

An interesting sidelight to the winning of this race is that the local Volvo dealer felt so confident about the Volvos winning the event he announced beforehand that he would offer a silver dollar to the leader of each lap in the race. In the end, both Jack and Bob Olthoff collected a pocketful of silver dollars; Olthoff had his made into a belt for his wife.

At the end of the 1963 season, and before the last race in the British Saloon Car Championship at Oulton Park, Jack had already been declared champion, which meant he could relax at the last round. The race also coincided with the world announcement of the Lotus-Cortina, and Colin Chapman was very keen to have two of them running in the final round of the championship.

Always one with an eye to commerce, Chapman realised that if the cars did well he might sell a few examples for racing the next season at his motor show coming up in October. Chapman contacted Walter Hayes, the brains behind the immensely successful Ford competition programme, including the Cosworth, to get him to agree that Jack Sears, the new British Saloon Car Champion with the Ford Cortina GT and Ford Galaxie, would drive a Lotus-Cortina in the final round, alongside his own works Formula Junior driver, Peter Arundell.

Comments Jack: "These were the A-bracket cars with the rear suspension in the shape of an A; handling was not actually as good as that of the Cortina GT. Also, I had already raced a Cortina GT at Oulton and the GT did not lift its front wheels but the A-bracket Lotus Cortina did. Coming into either a fast or a slow left-hander, the inside front wheel wanted to lift off the ground, which is why there are so many pictures of Jim Clark, Jackie Stewart, John Whitmore and myself with wheels off the ground. Much later on, in 1964, Colin Chapman eventually had to agree his A-bracket suspension was not really a good idea, so the Lotus Cortina went back to the Cortina GT rear suspension. Afterwards the car handled much better. It was one of Colin's mistakes.

"John Willment gave me permission to drive the Team Lotus car at Oulton and Graham Hill was asked to drive my normal Galaxie in the event. Graham was very fastidious and wanted to change this and that, whereas when Jim Clark had driven the Alan Brown Galaxie earlier in the year he just got into it, drove it, won and said 'lovely car, fantastic, I really enjoyed that.' Jimmy had the ability to drive through a car's idiosyncrasies as he was not an engineer, just a brilliant driver with incredible balance."

It was a successful debut as although Graham Hill won the race outright in the Willment Ford Galaxie with Sir

The Willment Ford Galaxie swept all before it. Jack Sears is seen here followed by a wildly understeering Jim Clark in the factory Lotus-Cortina. (Jack Sears Archive)

Gawaine Baillie second in his own Galaxie, Jack Sears took an incredible third place in the Lotus-Cortina. Jack and Peter Arundell finished first and second in the 1600cc Saloon Class, so proving the potential of the brand new Lotus-Cortina. Jack believes that he was given the Lotus Cortina drive following the remarkable duel he and Colin Chapman had had in their Jaguars at Silverstone some time before. Jack also found out about Lotus Cortinas lifting their front wheels, and remarked howt it always amused him when journalists enthused about how Jim Clark could race a Lotus Cortina with the front wheel way up of the ground, as though Jim Clark was the only one who could get the car to do this. As already noted, early Lotus Cortinas were apt to do this because of Chapman's suspension design.

John Willment sent Bob Olthoff and Frank Gardner to South Africa for the saloon car races in the annual Springbok Series. They took with them the Willment Cobra roadster, a Lotus Cortina, and the big Ford Galaxie. For the nine hour race at Kyalami, Jack Sears was sent out specifically to race the Galaxie with Paul Hawkins. The pair had an eventful race which ended prematurely with a blown cylinder head gasket; it was also the last event in Jack's full and successful 1963 motor racing season.

Jack Sears' involvement with Cobras is more inclusive than most people probably imagine, as he is the only racing driver who drove the AC Cobra in all its forms, from the original Cobra roadster through the one-off AC Cobra Coupé built by AC for Le Mans, the specially designed and built Willment Cobra Coupés, and finally the ultimate Shelby Cobra Daytona Coupé. The opening race meeting of the season at Snetterton took place in a downpour, the like of which few had ever seen before. The rain was so bad that, on race morning, the organisers gave a short open test period in which drivers could go out and adjust their cars to the conditions. It was at this race meeting that Graham Hill hit a puddle with his BRM and shot off the road and over an earth banking, and where a young Jackie Stewart had his first ever race in a single-seater annihilating the Formula Junior field in his Ken Tyrrell Cooper.

Jack Sears was entered for the Saloon Car race with John Willment's Ford Galaxie, and had Jack Brabham lined up against him driving Alan Brown's Ford Galaxie, with Jim Clark just behind in the Team Lotus Lotus Cortina. Sears set off in the lead from pole position: "I knew that Jack Brabham was very good in the wet and managed to get a reasonable margin on him, perhaps a hundred yards,

Jack Sears' Galaxie in action racing at the 9 hour Kyalami race, where he shared the car with Paul Hawkins. (Courtesy Rob Young)

One of the few photographs taken early in the morning on the M1 motorway service station, with the AC Cobra Coupé looking strange amongst the lorries. On this occasion, Jack clocked over 180mph and caused a furore in England. (Jack Sears Archive)

and then I became conscious of him beginning to catch me. I thought, that's okay, let's take that on board, don't panic, just drive your race. About halfway through the race I entered Richies Corner and there was a Mini ahead of me that I was about to lap. The Mini spun right in front of me; I couldn't avoid it and hit it for six with the front quarter of the Galaxie. The aluminium bumper was forced back onto the tyre so I couldn't steer the car. The marshals tried hard to get the bumper off the tyre with a crowbar so that I could get back to the pits, but I had to retire and Jack Brabham won the race with Jim Clark second."

A week later at Silverstone, Jack Sears and Dan Gurney met up with their Galaxies and this time Sears won the race on the full Grand Prix circuit, admitting afterwards it was one of the most satisfying race wins he had had in his career.

Despite the fact that Caroll Shelby was running a team of Shelby Cobras at Le Mans, the AC factory in England planned to design and build its own Coupe for Le Mans. By early May the car was in running condition and was taken to the Motor Industry Research Association banked test track for some initial high speed runs. Results were inconclusive; the problem being that, at the fastest point on the circuit, the car could achieve around 165mph only, meaning that AC needed more space to determine the terminal velocity of the smooth aerodynamic coupé. Someone in the party suggested the car be tested on the M1, Britain's first motorway. This was not as mad an idea as it appeared for not only were there no speed limits on the M1 at that time, it was also well known that both Jaguar and Aston Martin occasionally used the M1 for high speed testing. 1964 traffic density in England was virtually nothing compared to the stop-go nature of some areas today, so it was agreed that AC would take the car to one of the service areas on the M1 early one morning, when there was virtually no traffic on the road, and find out the car's true top speed.

On the appointed day Jack Sears and Peter Bolton, who were to race the car at Le Mans, turned up at dawn, around 4.00am. Jack, as usual, was dressed in his sports jacket and tie: "I never thought to dress in anything else, and if I was going to get arrested I may as well do it in style."

GENTLEMAN JACK

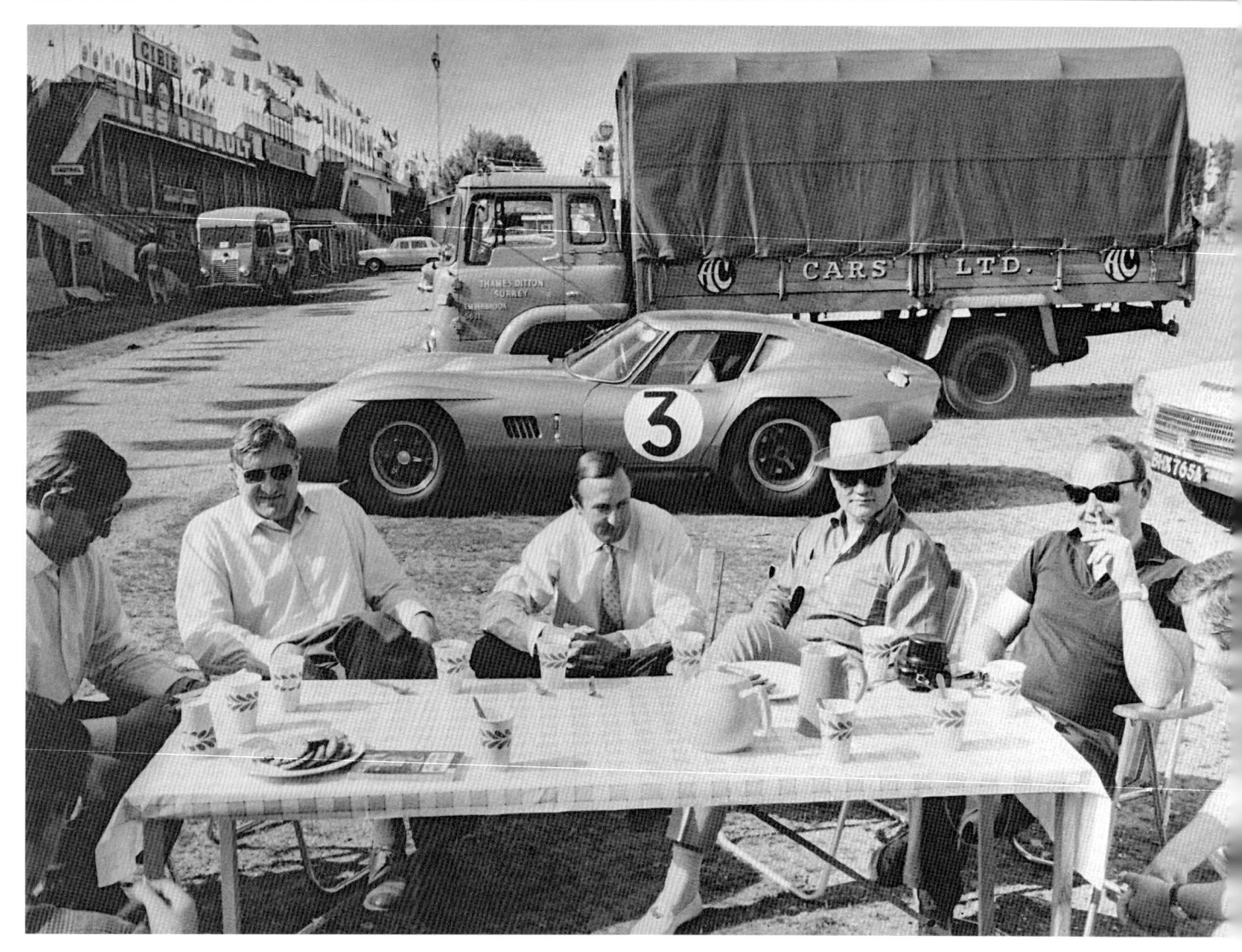

Le Mans: Jack Sears and Peter Bolton with the AC Coupé in the paddock at Le Mans. Second from the left is Derek Hurlock, Chairman of AC Cars Ltd, with Tony Martin on the extreme right. (Jack Sears Archive)

Jack remembers the occasion well, not only for reasons of the exercise but also the repercussions. "We all arrived as dawn was breaking, the birds were singing, and the car was unloaded from the transporter.

"I was to do the first run and we had two sets of wheels and tyres; one set with Goodyears, the other with Dunlops. The road was empty and you really could let the thing have its head. If I saw a car ahead I would back off so as not to give the fellow a fright, but I did get to the point where I knew the car simply would not go any faster. It just held its revs in top gear so I then looked for the next exit, came off the motorway, went over the bridge and back down the other side to return to the service station. When I spoke to the engineers and told them the revs I was holding in top they pulled out slide rules, not computers. They put in all the co-ordinates of the tyre size, etc, and worked out that the car was holding 185mph. Peter Bolton went out and did the same and by about 5.30am everything was finished. I was back home in a couple of hours having a jolly good breakfast, mission completed."

"One of the people in the team was a man called Tony Martin, the nephew of Derek Hurlock, owner of AC Cars. Martin worked for one of the big newspapers in Fleet Street, not as a journalist but on the administration side. After the test Tony returned to work, and later that morning went into one of the Fleet Street wine bars where all the journalists go. He mentioned to someone that he had just watched his uncle's car doing 185mph on the M1 that morning, and suddenly the story broke; as it was the silly season all of the papers carried this story on the front page. Questions were asked in the House of Commons and various organisations tut-tutted about it all. Then the phone began ringing; in the end I simply refused to talk to any more journalists. It really hit the headlines, just a few days before Le Mans."

Jack Sears left all the furore behind and travelled to Le Mans for the race. He and Peter Bolton set off in the race and everything seemed to be going well. The car was not as powerful as the Shelby cars but still managed to record over 180mph on the Mulsanne Straight. Jack then handed over to Peter Bolton, went to the motor caravan and fell asleep. He was awakened to be told that the car had crashed and was out; the AC had burst a tyre at high speed and gone off the road. Bolton was taken to hospital for observation and kept there overnight, mainly suffering from concussion.

The wreckage of the car was returned to the AC factory at Thames Ditton where it remained for many years until Barry Bird, a North Sea helicopter pilot, managed to acquire it on the understanding that he would restore it.

When Jack returned to England the controversy over the motorway incident was still in full swing, despite the fact that it had been perfectly legal as there was no speed limit on motorways at that time. The British Minister of Transport was the legendary left-wing firebrand, Barbara Castle, who, incidentally, didn't drive. The affair played into the hands of the zealots who felt that driving at that speed, albeit on an empty motorway, was irresponsible, and Jack Sears took the brunt of the criticism. When a 70mph speed limit was introduced on motorways three years later, the story was revived and Jack had to live with the suggestion that his escapade had been the cause of the 70mph limit. However, some years later, Tony Martin met Barbara Castle at a social event and asked her whether the story concerning his uncle's car, the AC Cobra Coupé, had had any affect on her decision to impose the speed limit. She was able to confirm that the government was already reviewing the speed limit before the test had taken place ...

More Cobras & the Brands Hatch Incident

The 1964 British Grand Prix meeting at Brands Hatch was a memorable one for Jack Sears as it marked one of the few occasions where he admits he totally lost his cool and ran the race in a total red mist. It turned out to be probably his greatest ever race, and one which finally underlined the fact that Jack was a true 'racer'.

On this occasion he was running in the Willment Cobra Roadster, and went out onto the circuit annoyed that he had only been fourth fastest in practice, putting him on the right side of the second row of the three-two-three grid. Ahead of him should have been Bob Olthoff's Cobra as Bob had established fastest time in practice; however, he crashed on the following lap and his car could not be repaired in time for the race. "I thought that's a stroke of luck for me" says Jack, "because I will have nobody ahead of me on the grid and a nice clear run into Paddock Bend."

In the centre of the front row was Jackie Stewart in John Coombs' lightweight E-type Jaguar, and on Stewart's left was

British GP GT support race; Jack in the Willment Cobra. (Jack Sears Archive)

Jack Sears is black flagged at Brands Hatch and comes into the pits (above). After a reprimand Sears sets off again, shaking his fist at all and sundry, whilst team manager, Jeff Uren, stomps back to the pit. (Jack Sears Archive)

Roy Salvadori in the Tommy Atkins Cobra. The cars were not lined up in the pit lane in practice order, and – for reasons he cannot remember – Jack left the pit lane further down the field. By the time he reached the grid a lot of cars were already in place, so he had to thread his way around to get to his second row position. When he reached his allotted spot he noticed that Jackie Stewart had now moved from the centre of the front row to pole position, and Roy Salvadori had moved into the middle, leaving a space on the front row to his left. Thinking that everyone had now moved up a place, Jack drove into the blank space on the front row and nobody said anything. The two minute siren sounded, then the one minute, and then a marshal tapped Jack on the shoulder and shouted that he should be back on the second row. Annoyed at this distraction right at the start, Jack shouted "It's too late." Totally unnerved at being accused of starting from the wrong place on the grid, Jack didn't make a good start. "At the end of the first lap I saw the black flag being waved with my number on it and couldn't work out what was going on. Was there something hanging off the car I hadn't noticed? I duly came in and stopped by my pit. An official told me I had started from the wrong place on the grid, this was my penalty, and now I could continue, which is when I went off down the pit road waving my fist and effing and blinding at everyone. I left in last place and I suppose they had given me what is known today as a stop-and-go penalty.

"I was so angry I think my first lap was around two seconds faster than my practice time, and I was eating people ahead of me, passing them left, right and centre. Luckily, it was a 25 lap race and by about lap 20 I was challenging and passing first David Piper in his Ferrari GTO and then Roy Salvadori in the Cobra. Ahead of me was just Jackie Stewart in the Jaguar so I switched my headlights on full beam to try and distract him. Suddenly – maybe Jackie made a mistake – I was on such a charge I saw a gap I might not have normally seen, took the lead and held it.

"I went on to win but was then hauled up in front of the Stewards who listened to my story and said they would not take any action in this instance. I had pointed out to them that both Jackie Stewart and Roy Salvadori had changed grid positions but they didn't take much notice of that. I said 'thank you' to the Stewards and, as I left the room, the Marquis of Camden, who was chairman of the Stewards, looked at me and said: 'It was a bloody good race'. Of all the races I ever did this was my best!"

Both pictures: Jackie Stewart (Coombs E-Type Jaguar) tries to hold off Jack Sears' Willment AC Cobra at Brands Hatch in 1964. (Author collection)

This was not the only incident to occur, however. Whilst Jack was out driving his boots off, John Willment, the entrant, was in the pits seething. He found the Deputy Clerk of the Course, Basil Tye, and began berating him for Jack's black flagging. The exchange culminated in Willment losing his temper and pushing Tye up against a wall. Willment was also taken to the Stewards, fined £400 and banned from attending races at Brands Hatch for six months.

Two weeks after this John Willment entered both of his Ford Cortina GTs for a saloon car race at Cascais, and the Cobra Roadster for

In the closing laps of the GT race supporting the British Grand Prix, Jack Sears catches a late-braking Jackie Stewart. (Author collection)

Jackie Stewart peers nervously in his mirrors as Jack Sears prepares to sweep past at Brands Hatch, in the eventful GT race won by Sears after a black flag incident. (Jack Sears Archive)

the GT race which was called the GP of Portugal. Jack flew out to the event but the Willment transporter went off the road on the way to the race and fell over on its side. It was not a serious accident; the truck was put back on the road and continued to Cascais. However, Bob Olthoff took the Cobra out for practice and, unknown to him or the crew, nobody had checked the oil, which had leaked out of the sump presumably when the transporter went off the road. The mechanics tried to get the car running but it blew its engine on the first lap of the race. Meanwhile, Olthoff and Sears raced their Cortina GTs and Jack chalked up another win.

Meanwhile, John Willment had had another idea and was well advanced with his plans to build his own 'Shelby' Cobra Coupé. The Willment Cobra project was an interesting one, a complete one-off exercise using a standard Shelby Cobra chassis. The men credited with the shape of the car were John Ohlsen, a New Zealander who had worked with Shelby on the original coupé, and Brian Waite. Ohlsen built the wooden buck before being recalled to the USA by Shelby, and the body itself was built in a small Twickenham garage by three ex-Aston Martin racing employees: Fred Shattock, Ted Richard and Geoff Gilbert. When Ohlsen left, his job was taken over by Frank Gardner. The chassis – CSX2131 – was supplied by Shelby. It proved a very successful car and is claimed to have competed in more races than any other Cobra coupé. It stayed with the team until 1967 when Willment ceased racing, and was sold to George Pitt and then raced by Amschel Rothchild. Eventually, however, it ended up in the United States.

Even Cobra Daytona Coupé designer, Peter Brock, in his book about the Shelby Daytona Coupés, admitted: "The Willment coupé's roofline is actually closer to my original design of the Daytona Coupé than the way we built CSX2287 [the original prototype]. We dropped the roofline at the high point for fear of not conforming with FIA regulations. John Willment evidently knew how they interpreted the rules and kept the roofline much flatter which possibly worked better than our car's."

When it was finished the car was taken to Snetterton where Frank Gardner and Jack Sears were entrusted with the shake-down.

The Willment Cobra Coupé was ready to race in time for the September 3 Hour International race meeting at Snetterton. Jeff Uren negotiated with Oliver Sear about starting money for the Coupé's debut race. Sear refused to pay the price Jeff Uren wanted, and it looked as though the Willment Coupé would not appear at the race until Sir William Bunbury, President of the Snetterton Racing Club, put his hand in his pocket and paid Oliver Sear the difference, simply to ensure the car had its debut at Snetterton.

In qualifying, the Cobra was well placed but, half an hour before the race started, there was a heavy rain storm and the track was soaked. However, the sun came out and partway through the race the temperature change caused fog to form. "I had been in for my refuelling stop and when I went out the fog got thicker at dusk. I seemed to be going like the wind and kept passing people. Finally, I was aware of a convoy of cars behind me, and whenever I passed someone he would tag on to the back of the convoy. It suddenly dawned on me that I seemed to be the only person who knew where he was going. After all, Snetterton was my home track and I had done several 24 hour runs round it in a variety of different cars – Morris Oxford, Morgan, Borgward – so I really knew the circuit backwards. I was beginning to think it was getting a bit silly because you couldn't really see very much, but I kept hammering on. Jeff Uren kept me informed so I knew I was in the lead by now. To my surprise I came round and saw 'P1 plus 1 lap': I had lapped the entire field so it didn't matter who passed me. The race was stopped twenty minutes early with me in first place."

The Ford Motor Company was, quite naturally, pleased as punch with the Ford Cortina's success, not only in winning the European Saloon Car Championship with Sir John Whitmore, but also all of the other successes it had achieved in rallies, racing, and even ice racing in Sweden, where Eric Berger had literally swept the field. Walter Hayes, Ford's director of public relations, arranged a private flight to Cortina d'Ampezzo in Italy and invited all of the people who had done well with Cortinas for a weekend of celebration.

Stuart Turner, later to become competitions manager of Ford, recalls a colleague telling him of an incident on this private flight. "On the flight down to Cortina the drivers tried to persuade one of the stewardesses to do a strip tease. They decided to have a whip-round, and when word of this got to the captain, the pilot came on to the tannoy and remarked: 'If you are getting Susan to do a strip put us in for 1/10 [11p in today's money].'"

Ford took over the best hotel but the highlight of the weekend was when Ford managed to arrange for the Olympic bobsleigh run to be opened specially for the drivers to take two Cortinas down. It was early December and the run had not yet been iced, but there were patches of snow and, of course, the banked corners were built up in concrete. Jack recalls that "All of the drivers had a go at this, and there was a link road from the bottom so you could drive back up to the top. Henry Taylor, for example, had been a member of the British bobsleigh team so had an advantage. It was a real fun weekend made notable by the fact that Jim Clark injured his arm in a snowball fight."

Once more Jack flew out to South Africa for the 9 hour saloon car race to share the driving of the Willment Cobra with Bob Olthoff. Despite the fact that they had to run in the open sports car Class, the Sears/Olthoff duo took fifth overall

More Cobras & the Brands Hatch incident

Which one looks the more uncomfortable, the young lady from Cortina d'Ampezzo or Jack Sears? (Jack Sears Archive)

Fun in the snow at Cortina d'Ampezzo. Jack, left, with Jim Clark, Henry Taylor and David Siegle-Morris. (Courtesy Ford Motor Co)

Cortina capers: Jack Sears at the wheel of a Ford Cortina on the famous Cortina bob-run. (Courtesy Ford Motor Co)

83

Snowball fight at Cortina, pelting the RAC's Dean Delamont (foreground). Facing him are (left to right): Ford racing and rally drivers, Vic Elford, Colin Chapman, Jack Sears, Eric Jackson, David Siegle Morris, and Jim Clark. (Courtesy Ford Motor Co)

and became great heroes. As the Willment Cobra Coupé had also been sent to South Africa, Bob Olthoff came up with the idea of trying to set a new South African Land Speed Record. The trouble was finding somewhere to make the attempt. Olthoff approached the manager of Cape Town International Airport with a view to using the main runway, which was five kilometres long. As they were aiming for a flying kilometre, it meant they had around two kilometres of space in which to build up

Jim Clark presents Jack Sears with a prize at the Ford Cortina event held at Cortina d'Ampezzo. Ford's Walter Hayes checks his notes. (Jack Sears Archive)

More Cobras & the Brands Hatch incident

The Kyalami 9 Hour race in South Africa. Jack thunders round in the Willment Cobra. He finished 5th overall. (Courtesy Rob Young)

speed, and then two kilomeres to slow down. Bob had hoped to clock 200mph but the space was just not long enough. He did one run and clocked 177mph but decided to abort the attempt. Olthoff was eventually to set a new record in 1967 using a stretch of the Soutpan Road near Bloemfontein. The car used was the ex-David Prophet McLaren-Elva, and Olthoff averaged 177.97mph with a single run of 182mph. By the time he stopped racing, Bob Olthoff had won 140 races to become South Africa's most successful racing driver – apart, that is, from Jody Scheckter who is South Africa's only World Motor Racing Champion.

Back in Norfolk, Jack's wife, Cicely, also had a busy time coping with three young children. The eldest, David, celebrated his ninth birthday during the Cortina trip and the girls, Suzanne and Jennifer, were beginning to become fascinated by the string of racing drivers that visited the house. As Suzanne recalled: "Lots of people came to stay and Tommy Sopwith used to bring glamorous women, which I suppose was hardly surprising, but we took it all for granted. We also got to know Innes Ireland, Jim Clark and Michael Parkes, who often came to stay, and we were thrilled. Also, dad resurrected the Atco car his grandmother had bought for him. It was a sweet little car and my sister and I learned to drive it."

Jack Sears was under contract with John Willment for the 1963 and 1964 seasons only, and at the end of 1964 Walter Hayes of the Ford Motor Company offered Jack a factory contract with Ford for the 1965 season. In effect it was a two-point agreement; the first being a contract alongside Jim Clark to race the Team Lotus factory entries in the British Saloon Car Championship, the second a contract to drive for Carroll Shelby's Cobra team in the World GT Championship.

For the assault on the GT Championship Ford had arranged for Alan Mann to co-ordinate and run the European effort with two cars, and Carroll Shelby to oversee the entire

GENTLEMAN JACK

Cicely and Jack Sears. (Jack Sears Archive)

American programme. It is interesting to note that all of the individual official Shelby American Daytona Coupés, save the prototype, were raced at one time or another by Alan Mann in 1965. Jack Sears' co-driver in the events would be Sir John Whitmore, and in addition to the Coupés would be a Shelby American Cobra roadster.

The 1965 season's opener for Jack, however, was at Sebring where there was a three hour saloon car race the day before the International 12 Hour sports car event. Colin Chapman was very keen to win this race as the BMWs were winning everything in American saloon car events. "Colin got Jim Clark and me together and told us he wanted us to go over there and win the race. As it was a single driver event – in those days we never thought anything about having to drive for three hours in a race – we would each have Lotus Cortinas."

Sears and Clark duly flew from London to Miami where they picked up their hire car, which turned out to be a Ford Galaxie. "At that time the speed limit on the interstate highway running north from Miami was 55mph. I knew Jimmy didn't like to be driven so I told him I would be so happy if he drove as I thought he was a pretty competent driver! He seemed relieved at that so I sat back and pulled down my sun visor, as we had agreed that Jimmy would probably not stick to 55mph so I would use my sun visor mirror to look out for traffic police. In a long, boring drive Jimmy wasn't doing 55mph but nearer 75, but we thought we were being very observant. Suddenly, we heard this wailing siren and, of course, there was a bloody police car behind us with everything flashing and all hell let loose. Jimmy said: 'Oh shit we had better stop'. The police car stopped in front of us and we both got out and walked toward the officer, who asked who had been driving. Jimmy admitted he was the driver and was told to come closer so I walked along with him. At this the policeman pointed at me and said: 'You ... you get back to the car'. Jimmy came back after a few minutes and told me it was a $50 fine, which we agreed to split 50/50. By this time the cop had cooled off sufficiently for me to ask him how he had manged to catch us as we were using our mirrors fairly diligently. He said he had followed us for a few miles, overtaking when we did.

"He asked where we were going and, when told Sebring, asked if we were race fans. We agreed we were as he obviously didn't know Jimmy or me. He then enquired if we knew a guy called 'jendybean'. Obviously, he meant Belgian driver Olivier Gendebien, so we told him we did. 'I caught him speeding one day a few years back but he couldn't speak English. We weren't getting very far at all so I had to take him down to the sheriff's office. I told the sheriff all about his speeding and the sheriff said 'If he doesn't speak English we got to get through to him it's a $100 fine'. As soon as the sheriff said $100 fine you ain't never heard anyone speak English so damn fast!'"

In practice for the three hour race Jim Clark was fastest

with Jack Sears second. Says Jack: "Jimmy took the lead in the race. I tried to keep with him but he kept edging away all the time: that man was just something out of this world; he had this extraordinary balance and just kept easing further and further away. I was quite pleased as I was in second and keeping ahead of the BMWs." The two Lotus Cortinas continued in this order to the end, which meant that Clark and Sears had done exactly what Colin Chapman and the Ford Motor Company wanted them to.

A new character entered Jack Sears' racing life at this point: Alan Mann. Alan Mann's involvement with motor racing stretched back to 1956 when he bought the ex-Ted Whiteaway HWM-Alta. The following year he ventured abroad and raced the car in the Naples Grand Prix that was won by Peter Collins in a Lancia-Ferrari, but suffered engine problems. As he didn't have enough spares, Mann had to withdraw his entry for the 1957 Monaco Grand Prix. When the formula for 1958 stipulated pump fuel, Alan couldn't afford to convert his Alta engine: by this time the car was getting a bit long in the tooth but he used it for hill climbs still.

Mann then worked with Roy Pierpoint at his garage at Rusper in Sussex and, in 1960, acquired the famous works 3.5 litre HWM-Jaguar, registration HWM 1. When he moved to Shoreham in Sussex to run a Ford dealership, he acquired a new Rolls-Royce V8 engine and, with Alan Mann's help, built a rear-engined sports car known as the Rolls-Royce Marina. However, in practice for the Guards Trophy at Brands Hatch the rear suspension collapsed, from which point Alan had no confidence in the car and never raced it again.

For the first *Motor* 6 Hour race at Brands Hatch, Alan "... prepared a 1300cc Ford Anglia and, with Tony Hegbourne as co-driver, managed 2nd place in our Class."

Alan Mann's preparation and organization was respected everywhere, and his team went on to win the European Touring Car Championship in 1965 with Sir John Whitmore at the wheel of the Lotus-Cortina.

In the early 1960s, American racing legend, Carroll Shelby, had already carved a name for himself with the Shelby Cobra roadsters prepared by Phil Remington. The roadster, however, had a problem; aerodynamics. The key to a car's speed in a straight line is the manner in which the air passes over it. With the original Cobra roadsters the air met the rectangular front of the car as though hitting a brick wall, and although the Cobra had plenty of power to spare, this aerodynamic weakness was always going to make it inferior to the fluidly-shaped Ferrari GTO.

This realisation prompted Carroll Shelby to suggest to his number two, Peter Brock, who had worked in the GM design studio, to look at improving the aerodynamics of the Cobra roadster, which gave Brock the chance to develop what, for many people, is the ultimate Cobra, the Shelby American Coupé.

At this juncture it's worth pointing out that the Ford V8-engined AC sports car was called the Cobra by Shelby, and in the FIA homologation papers for the car, and the subsequent Coupé, the manufacturer was always Shelby American, Inc, Venice, California. Technically, the anglicised 'AC-Cobra' never existed; it was always the Shelby Cobra and the Shelby Cobra Daytona Coupé.

Throughout 1963 Brock and Phil Remington worked on the Coupé project, and it was tested by Ken Miles for the first time in February 1964. When asked what it would be called, Shelby came up with 'Daytona', and promised the car would make its debut at the Florida circuit just two weeks later!

During the 1964 season the Daytona Coupé was developed and raced with great success. At Sebring it won the GTIII Class, and the Class at the Goodwood Tourist Trophy race. Most significantly, it won the GT Class at the Le Mans 24 Hour race driven by Dan Gurney and Bob Bondurant. At the end of the season Ferrari did win the GT Championship from the Shelby Coupés by just 6 points. Clearly, this was the Ferrari-beater Carroll Shelby had dreamed: the stage was set for the World GT Championship the following year.

The Shelby American Cobra Coupé Programme

Shelby American had just five months to develop and prepare a raft of cars for the 1965 racing season. The team now had the full might of Ford behind it as Shelby American had been given the Ford GT40 programme to deal with. The concept was that the Ford GT40s would be seeking outright wins in the prototype Class at tracks like Le Mans and the Cobra Coupés would be looking for GT category wins in as many as possible of the FIA events.

Nice theory, but in practice designer Peter Brock found his Cobra Coupé programme sidelined as Ford descended upon Shelby American to give the Ford GT40 programme the top priority. As a result a Mark II Coupé concept was shelved and attention turned to the existing six 1964 Cobra Coupés in preparation for Daytona in 1965; this also meant that the GT40 programme would suck up all the best international drivers. Bob Bondurant was to be the lead American driver in the Cobra team, which went to Daytona and Sebring and won the GT Category at both, so leading the GT World Championship before moving to Europe.

However, there was a problem; the cost of the Ford GT40 programme meant that there was little or no budget with which to continue with the GTs. Ray Geddes of Ford Europe realised that by coming to Europe and continuing in the FIA GT Championship, Ford would benefit from a boost in European markets. As Alan Mann was at Sebring, a meeting with Shelby, Geddes and John Wyer – team manager of the Ford GT40 effort – was arranged, at which it was decided that the GT programme would be transferred to Alan Mann Racing for the rest of the season.

Alan Mann had just finished the Monte Carlo Rally where he had run the Ford Falcon Futura Sprints. As part of the deal it was agreed that he could keep the huge pile of spare parts and the Falcon rally cars in part payment for taking over the Shelby Daytona Cobra Coupé assault from Monza onward. This meant Mann had consigned to him not only two cars, but also free use of the rest of the Shelby American Cobra Coupé inventory. There would be two American drivers in the team, Bob Bondurant and Alan Grant, and chief mechanic, Charlie Agapiou, would join them in England. The only future link between Shelby American and the Cobra Coupé programme would be Le Mans, where Shelby would run his own cars alongside the Alan Mann-entered cars.

Bob Bondurant's contract stated he was number one driver in the Alan Mann-run team, but when he met Alan Mann at London airport he was told that Alan had signed Sir John Whitmore and Jack Sears for the team, and that they would be numbers one and two with Bondurant number three. Mann added that he wanted Bondurant to know this from the start so that he could fly back to the USA if he did not agree. Bondurant whipped out his contract with Carroll Shelby but was countered by Alan Mann who showed Bondurant *his* contract with Ford Motor Company, which gave Mann control over the drivers he ran in his team.

Bondurant agreed to stay with the team but was clearly not at all happy about this situation. As Peter Brock wrote in *Daytona Cobra Coupés*, co-authored with Dave Friedman and George Stauffe: "Shelby had cautioned Mann not to let Bondurant and Grant compromise his bid for the championship by allowing the American drivers to run flat out for their personal glory."

For Jack Sears this was a tremendous opportunity and he relished the fact that he would be sharing a car with his friendly rival, Sir John Whitmore. Obviously, Jack knew about

Practice at the Tourist Trophy Race, Oulton Park, 1966. Jack bends down to check on the tyres whilst Shell competitions manager, Brian Turle, left, looks on. (Author collection)

Different attitudes. Jack Sears oversteers his Lotus Cortina out of Club Corner at Silverstone, whilst team-mate, John Whitmore, shows marked understeer. (Author collection)

Carroll Shelby and his reputation and had great respect for what he had done in motor racing up to that time. "As an avid *Autosport* reader I had seen photographs of Carroll Shelby racing in the United States and Europe, and was particularly impressed when he won the 1959 Le Mans 24 Hour race with my friend, Roy Salvadori, in an Aston Martin DBR1. As a farmer I was also amused at the way he raced back then in his striped chicken farm overalls, which apparently brought him luck. Also, when out of a car he always wore a black Stetson hat and had the air of the laconic western film star. Little did I know that one day I would actually be racing in the Shelby Cobra Daytona Coupé team.

"I did not actually meet Carroll until Le Mans in 1965, when he brought his own team of Cobra Daytona Coupés to race alongside our Alan Mann cars. However, our friendship blossomed many years later, after I had retired, through the annual Shelby reunion which is held at the Shelby Collection Museum at Boulder, Colorado every December. Much as I expected, Carroll is a tall, larger-than-life character with an infectious sense of humour and full of stories. His heart problems caused him to stop racing and, later, he was to have a heart transplant; he established the Shelby Heart Foundation that has raised many millions of dollars for heart research. Today, at 84 years of age, he amusingly remarks that he may be 84 but he has the heart of a 51 year old!"

The first European round of the World Manufacturer's GT Championship was scheduled for Monza, and the two Shelby Daytona Coupés arrived in Milan in April: Jack Sears and Sir John Whitmore would drive chassis CSX 2602 and Bob Bondurant and Alan Grant chassis CSX2601. Both cars – the fourth and fifth Daytona Coupés to be built – had bodies by Carrozzeria Gransport in Modena. The Bondurant/Grant car had finished second at Sebring whilst the Whitmore/Sears car was the second-placed Daytona car.

Alan Mann had been given the responsibility of not only running the cars in Europe but running them to win the World Manufacturers' GT Championship. As a manufacturers' championship the drivers were not important: getting to the finishing line, being driven as consistently as possible to maintain the GT Class lead, and finishing high enough to gain points was. This was the job that Alan Mann was asked to do by Ford and Shelby and this was the job he did with great skill and acumen. Indeed, Alan Mann, a down-to-earth individual, instilled in all his drivers that they were not there to improve their CVs but to chauffeur the cars round and ensure that the Cobras beat the Ferraris, as Ferrari had won the Championship for the previous three years with the GTO.

The strategy Mann followed was to analyse the practice results to decide a lap time considered to be an ideal balance between performance and reliability to win the race, and the drivers would run to that strategy.

Generally speaking, when it came to the actual races, Sears and Whitmore stuck to the lap times but, on occasion, Bob Bondurant would appear to forget the plan and go charging off into the distance. This did not wear well with Alan Mann because, apart from disobeying team orders, the long distance reliability of the car could be affected, compromising the objective of getting the cars to the finish and scoring points at all costs.

The Monza course that year included the notorious banked sections which, even when they were new, were rough and bumpy. For Jack Sears it was an interesting challenge as it was not the first time he had been on a banked circuit. He recalled a day in 1939 when his father decided to test a Bentley saloon round Brooklands and took Jack, at the tender age of 9, and his brother, Eric, along with the Bentley factory representative. Jack had been impressed by the Brooklands banking but with Monza he was enthusiastic: "... the banking at Monza rather turned me on and I thought it quite dramatic to see the horizon changing ... I rather liked the banking, and it certainly made Monza an interesting circuit."

In practice the thundering Daytonas were a full 14 seconds faster than the nearest Ferrari GT, and so a softly-softly approach was adopted to save the cars from a real drubbing on the banking. Bondurant's time, however, was a full 8 seconds a lap faster than Whitmore's and quicker than a number of prototypes, including some Ford GT40s.

The race started in predictable fashion with Bondurant and Whitmore going hammer and tongs. Alan Mann held out the slow signal and both cars obeyed; Bondurant kept being given the 'EZ' signal whereas Whitmore and Sears slowed so much that John Whitmore remarked "... we actually ran slower in the race than the two litre Alfa Romeos. It was quite frustrating because we knew we should have been in the hunt. However, If we hadn't followed this plan, we would have shaken the cars apart on the banking, and ourselves, too."

Alan Mann added maximum points to the Daytona and Sebring scores in the FIA GT Championship and immediately began preparing for the next race at Oulton Park, the Tourist Trophy. As this was a week after Monza and the Coupés had to be prepared for the Spa race, another Cobra Coupé was flown over from the United States to run at Oulton Park. This car was CSX2299, the 1964 Le Mans-winning vehicle. As Mann was contracted to run two cars, the Cobra Roadster was brought into play for John Whitmore to drive, whilst Jack Sears was given the Cobra Coupé.

The TT that year was run in two heats; the prototype Class had a stellar field with Jim Clark in the factory Lotus 30, Bruce McLaren in his McLaren, and John Surtees with his Lola T70.

In practice Jack Sears was quickest of the GT cars with a

time of 1:46.6. After practice Alan Mann told John Whitmore to let Jack go, but if Jack had any problems then to push ahead. Whitmore got his chance sooner than expected as Sears' Daytona Coupé simply refused to start. As he had to be push-started, Sears received a two-lap penalty. On the warm-up lap the brakes began to act up and so Jack came into the pits. A broken balance bar was repaired and Sears set off at his usual 110 per cent pace.

Jack Sears is a meticulously organised man; during preparation of this book he would outline exactly what we would do each day and would get irritated if I changed the subject. His concentration levels are quite remarkable, and he has proved throughout his career to be probably one of the greatest 'team' drivers anyone could wish for; he obeyed orders and, if the car was right, would wring its neck in a race. He once quietly explained to me that in motor sport there were drivers and racers; he saw himself as a racer and proved it on many occasions. One such was at this Oulton Park TT for, when he went back out onto the track, he was electric, and kept breaking the GT lap record.

Meanwhile, in the race John Whitmore, following orders, took the lead in the GT Class but the car was dipping and wallowing all over the place and clearly something was wrong. Not only that but carbon monoxide fumes were drifting into the cockpit and he began to feel drowsy. The mechanical problem turned out to be a broken front anti-roll bar. Peter Sutcliffe won the first heat with his Ferrari GTO, the first Ferrari win in the season so far.

Jack Sears was clearly about to stamp his authority in the second heat and set a blistering pace, so much so that he was holding third place behind David Hobbs in a Lola T70 and Denny Hulme in the Brabham. Sears went on to win the GT Class with ease but his poor performance in the first heat meant he did not win the aggregate GT Class. Meanwhile, John Whitmore in the roadster struggled, but once more the quick-thinking Alan Mann had devised a plan to help him.

It was decided that Whitmore would not make a pit stop for fuel. The plan worked – but only just: a mere two pints of petrol remained in the tank at the finish and one of the tyres was down to the canvas. Only Mann and Whitmore were aware of this plan to run without a pit stop and, in order to fool the Ferrari drivers (including Michael Parkes in the Maranello Concessionaires GTO '64), Mann even held out the 'In' sign to Whitmore with five laps to go, which John ignored, as planned. Whitmore won the GT Class and gave Mann the welcome points he needed.

As the next FIA GT Championship event was at Spa a week later, and as this was a single driver event, Sir John Whitmore drove his Monza car and Bondurant drove the Monza Class winner. Jack Sears' next race was, therefore, the 1000km of the Nürburgring.

It is often forgotten that Alan Mann was probably one of the finest team tacticians in motor racing. Others, like Neubauer of Mercedes Benz and John Wyer of Gulf Racing, are lauded to the heights, but if you look closely at the manner in which Alan Mann ran his motor racing teams in the 1960s he was clearly a few brain cells ahead of most of his opposition. He was a man who thought on his feet, as his Oulton Park decision proved, and he moulded a team in which both drivers and mechanics trusted him implicitly. I caught a brief glimpse of this during the 1965 Monte Carlo Rally when, with American journalists, Henry Manney III and Jerry Sloniger, I was given a behind-the-scenes view of Alan Mann's organisation, in which nothing was left to chance. Indeed, Mann was so well organised that he was able to re-route two of his mechanics to guard a 'short cut' they had found on one of the special stages, just to make sure that nobody used it on the event.

Spa was an ideal circuit for the slippery Shelby Daytona Coupés, and John Whitmore set up second fastest overall time to Michael Parkes' factory Ferrari 330P prototype, with Willy Mairesse in the 250LM equalling Whitmore's time. As usual, in the pits, Alan Mann was looking for GT wins only and was not the slightest bit interested in an overall win: but John Whitmore and Bob Bondurant had different ideas. They were lying second and third overall behind Mairesse when Whitmore was blocked by a back marker and ran into the back of him. This let Bondurant into second place overall but the battle between the two Cobras had left its mark. Bondurant's car went on to seven cylinders but he managed to finish second in the GT Class to Peter Sutcliffe's Ferrari GTO.

The GT programme was hectic as there was just a week before the cars had to appear at Nürburgring for the 1000kms race. For this race the team had new faces: Bob Bondurant was paired with Nürburgring specialist, Jochen Neerpasch, and Jack Sears was paired with Australian Frank Gardner. Alan Mann was also given an additional budget by Ford to run a third car, which was quickly flown over from Shelby American to be driven by Jo Schlesser and Andre Simon.

Apart from fresh engines, the Alan Mann Shelby Daytona Coupés were the same cars as had raced at Spa, the body damage to Whitmore's car hastily repaired. There was another change. When Alan Mann signed his contract with Ford there hadn't been a separate tyre contract; Shelby American was under contract to Goodyear but Alan Mann was free to use any tyres he wished. He briefly tried Firestones in practice at Spa but these were not as good as the Goodyears. However, after back-to-back tests of the Goodyears and some new Firestones on the 'hack' Shelby Cobra Roadster at Nürburgring, the team chose to run on Firestone tyres.

In qualifying the Shelby Cobra Daytona Coupés left

the Ferraris for dead, Bob Bondurant setting a time that was over eighteen seconds faster than the existing GT lap record established by a GTO the previous year. Indeed, all three Cobras were below the record. The Bondurant/Neerpasch car was clearly the quickest and led the way to win the Class, with Jack Sears and Frank Gardner in second place and the Schlesser/Simon car in third.

The nucleus of everyone's attention, however, was Le Mans 1965, for which Ford entered four GT40s and two Mark IIs. Five Shelby Daytona Coupés were entered for the GT Class – none by Alan Mann. Ford France put up one; Shelby-American two; Scuderia Fillipinetti one, and the fifth, strangely enough, was entered by AC Cars. However, this latter entry was merely a technicality to appease the French organisers. Alan Mann's organisational skills and team were brought in to run the GT assault at Le Mans. Mann also lost two of his drivers to the Ford GT effort, with John Whitmore and Bob Bondurant switching to the prototypes.

A surprise entry was a Ferrari 275GTB/S from Ecurie Francorchamps. Ferrari had convinced the FIA that the 275GTB was a series production GT car, and here it was replacing the Ferrari GTOs. It seemed that, for once, the Ferrari team would not get its way as the notorious Le Mans scrutineers went over the car with a fine tooth comb, pointing out where it differed from the road car, particularly in terms of its weight. The arguments went on but, eventually, the car was allowed to run.

The race was a disaster for Ford as not one of the Ford prototypes finished. The Shelby Cobra Daytona Coupés were also affected – mainly by problems with cylinder head gaskets – and all of them retired, save the car driven by Jack Sears and American dentist Dick Thompson. When it was running, the fastest of the Shelby Cobra Daytona Coupés, driven by Dan Gurney and Jerry Grant, was far faster than any of the other GT cars, but when the Shelby Cobra Daytona Coupés began to drop out it was the Ferrari 275GTB/S that took the lead, finishing in third place overall, a remarkable performance.

The Sears car was dogged by oil pressure problems and kept pitting, thereafter having to be driven at a slower pace for the rest of the race. It must have been an interminable slog round Le Mans at a slower than usual speed just to finish, but finish they did, in 8th place, to take second place in the GT Class. Thompson and Sears had obeyed team orders, struggling on through the long night to finish (theirs was the only Ford-powered car to finish the race that year). Despite the fact that Ford returned 1966 to totally dominate the 24 Hours of Le Mans, the 1965 result will go down in history as the blackest day in Ford Motor Company's racing history.

An incident occurred in the Alan Mann pit after the race. Graham Hill – who had been driving the Rover Gas Turbine car with Jackie Stewart – came over to apologise to Jack for when the two cars touched at White House due to the fact that the Turbine engine had hesitated at the wrong moment. Recalls Jack: "What actually happened was I came up to lap Graham at high speed. Suddenly, his car slowed and, in passing him on the corner, our cars brushed together, leaving green paint on the side of my Cobra. We were lucky not to have a serious accident on such a dangerous corner."

Alan Mann's grip on the FIA GT Championship lead, despite the Ferrari Class win that carried double points at Le Mans, was not seriously challenged and, with just two races to go, could be safely buttoned up barring any other 'incidents'. The problem with the engines at Le Mans had been traced to a relatively simple mistake in their build, and so Alan Mann decided to enter just two Shelby Cobra Daytona Coupés for the 12 Hour race on the fast Reims circuit in France (a high speed circuit ideally suited to the Cobras). One of the cars left in England before Le Mans was brought to France, and the other was the Allan Grant car from Le Mans that had retired with a broken clutch.

The old internecine race problems once more intervened. Bob Bondurant and his co-driver, Jo Schlesser, wanted to go out and win at all costs but Alan Mann wanted his number one team of John Whitmore and Jack Sears as the leaders. It was not a happy race for the team as Schlesser and Bondurant wanted to race with the prototypes rather than be told to stay behind the Whitmore/Sears car. However, after about eight hours of racing, Jack Sears brought his Cobra into the pits with serious engine problems.

Alan Mann and the mechanics decided that they had to isolate one cylinder and the car continued on seven cylinders. The late French journalist, Jabby Crombac, who was Clerk of the Course and organiser of the Reims race, saw what was going on at the pit stop and bet Alan Mann a hundred bottles of champagne that the car would never finish. However, Sears and Whitmore not only managed to continue, just in case something should happen to the Bondurant car, but did, in fact, finish and Alan Mann collected his hundred bottles of champagne from Crombac.

This problem with the Sears and Whitmore car released Bondurant and Schlesser from their bond, and they romped home winners of the GT Class, which also confirmed the FIA World Manufacturers' GT Championship for the Shelby Cobra Daytona Coupé team. The crippled Sears/Whitmore car took second place, the only finisher in the GT Class!

The final race at Enna in Sicily was an anti-climatic nightmare with Bondurant finishing third overall, slowed because of tyre wear. Jack Sears trundled round to finish second in the GT Class.

To a driver like Sears, who believed in discipline and obeying team orders, one senses that it was a rewarding, but at the same time sad, season in which he had to contend

Just to prove it was possible to do almost anything with a Lotus Cortina. (Jack Sears Archive)

with petty squabbles and the whiff of corporate-based motor racing as practiced by the Ford Motor Company in the 1960s. His other races in 1965 were altogether much happier in what could be termed a British milieu.

At the end of the season there was time for reflection. Charlie Agapiou, who been sent over from Shelby American and grafted into the Alan Mann team, arrived unknown and not knowing anybody but, by the end of the season, had some specific views about the two English drivers, particularly Jack Sears. As quoted by Peter Brock, Charlie remarked: "Jack Sears was such a smooth driver that you really never realised just how fast he was going, and he went very fast. Jack was also the best driver that I ever worked with regarding following team and mechanics' orders."

Despite his commitment to the Alan Mann/ Shelby programme, in 1965 Jack was still heavily involved in British racing as a member of Colin Chapman's official Team Lotus entry for the British Saloon Car Championship. For the British Grand Prix support race, Colin Chapman had to find a replacement for Jim Clark who was not allowed to race as he was in the Grand prix proper. He chose Sir John Whitmore and the ground was laid for an epic duel.

Sears and Whitmore were fellow farmers, and had been friends since 1959 when Whitmore, as a virtual unknown, qualified his Lotus Elite on the second row of the grid at Silverstone alongside Jack. As John Whitmore remarks: "I used to rib Jack quite a bit and told him he was the one who should have been 'Sir'" and not me because, at the time, I was such a rebel and he was the perfect gentleman." Now here they were at Silverstone in identical factory Lotus Cortinas.

Jack Sears well remembers the situation: "Now, you must understand, I didn't want to be beaten by John and he didn't want to be beaten by me. We regarded ourselves as equals and it was a matter of honour. We qualified within a hundredth of a second of each other and were behind the Mustangs on the grid.

"We duelled side-by-side for the first five laps, really going

Who says Jim Clark was the only person to three-wheel a Lotus Cortina? Jack Sears reaches new heights at Crystal Palace. (Jack Sears Archive)

at it, passing and re-passing, with Colin Chapman on the pit counter ruling everything, as he did with his Grand Prix cars. He leaned over and gave the signal that I knew meant we were to ease up and not take each other out. So on the next lap on Hanger Straight I lifted off a little and John came alongside. I then tucked my knees under the steering wheel, lifted my hands off and indicated to John that we should try and make it a dead heat. John nodded, understanding exactly what I meant and so we immediately began lapping about two seconds a lap slower, which pleased Colin no end. Then we continued to pass and re-pass every lap so that nobody knew exactly what was going on.

"Finally, we came up to Woodcote on the last lap. I was on the inside and John was on the outside and we were looking across at each other as we entered the corner a bit slower, but side-by-side, and crossed the line. John was still looking at me and suddenly realised he was now flat out on the grass on the exit of Woodcote. He went the entire length of the pit straight on the grass in his Lotus Cortina, teasing it gently back onto the track again, with me moving over to try and give him room. Honour was satisfied when the timekeepers and Judges of Fact on the finish line gave us the dead heat we wanted."

There was another occasion when Sears and Whitmore were asked to stage a dead heat, but which did not come off. When Alan Mann entered Whitmore and Sears in a Lotus

Sears and Whitmore again demonstrate contrasting styles at Silverstone in Lotus-Cortinas. (Author collection)

Cortina for the six hour saloon car race at the Nürburgring in June, he knew they had a good chance of success. However, Mann had also entered his Ford Mustang for Roy Pierpoint and local German hero, Jochen Neerpasch. In the race Whitmore had the first driving stint and the Lotus Cortina took the lead, which Sears kept, with Whitmore taking the final stint.

"We were a hell of a long way in front, a seriously long way," says Jack "and suddenly there was a call to try and contrive a dead heat between the Lotus-Cortina and the Mustang. Neither John nor I thought that was quite fair and were determined to keep our lead. My recollection of the situation was that the two cars closed up and, at the very last second, John gave the car that last push and won by a tenth of a second. In the record books the outright winner was the Whitmore/Sears Lotus Cortina with the Pierpoint/Neerpasch Ford Mustang in second place because I felt that after we had built up a lead to then reduce it to a dead heat was really not very fair."

Throughout the season Jack Sears had also been acting as test driver for Colin Chapman with the Lotus-Cortinas and is quick to point out that he tested both his own car and Jim Clark's. Whereas the story goes that Clark always had a better car than the second team driver, Sears can confirm that there was absolutely no difference between the two factory Lotus-Cortinas. However, Colin was clearly happy with the result of Jack's ability to translate problems from testing that Colin could work on, so asked if Jack would be prepared to do some test driving of the Lotus 30. Jack saw this as a bit of a challenge and admits that the Lotus 30, with its 4.7 litre Ford V8 engine, was actually the quickest car he had driven and it took a little time to get used to its idiosyncrasies. The test programme was almost always located at Snetterton – Jack's home circuit – which he knew

At the Guards Trophy in August 1964 Jack won the GT Class with the Willment AC Cobra Roadster. Jack is more interested in film star, Susan Hampshire, than the crowd, or Bruce McLaren, who won the sports car Class. (Jack Sears Archive)

like the back of his hand. His original Lotus 30 test occurred in April 1965, but in May Colin was sufficiently impressed to offer Jack a race in the car at the International Trophy meeting at Silverstone. Jack was already down to race the Team Lotus Lotus-Cortina but took over Jim Clark's Lotus 30 as Jim was tied up in America qualifying for Indianapolis.

The 25-lap sports car race pulled a superb entry, including Bruce McLaren in the factory McLaren-Oldsmobile, who took the lead from the start but was harried by John Surtees in his Lola-Chevrolet T70 and Jack Sears with the Lotus 30. John Surtees made his lunge at Stowe and claimed the lead. Then, as he and Bruce McLaren were about to lap Julian Sutton's Attila-Chevrolet, Sutton's car shed a wheel and Surtees took to the grass to avoid being hit. Though he held the sliding Lola and got back on the track, the damage was done as the car had broken a water pipe and pulled up a few laps later with steam everywhere. Bruce McLaren went on to win with Hugh Dibley's Lola in second place and Jack Sears third in the Lotus 30.

The Lotus 30 has always had a bad name, but Jack Sears is remarkably positive about it. "I only raced the car once as Jimmy raced it most of the time. The car was really designed and built for him to go out and beat the Lola T70s and the McLarens. Unfortunately, even with Jimmy's innate skill, he couldn't succeed. However, I enjoyed driving it and felt I was master of the car, though it just didn't seem to handle well enough to compete with the Lolas and McLarens."

Some time later Frank Gardner gave an even more dramatic description of the Lotus 30. "... Willment had one which I drove, and it was quite a good one which had all kinds of good money spent on it. I was racing the thing at Zeltweg when the bloody chassis broke clean in two in the closing stages, and I brought it home second with the thing darting and weaving in all directions, hingeing in the middle!

"It also had aerodynamic problems, and after poor old Jack Sears really crooked himself testing a Lotus 40 at Silverstone, Lotus asked me to get some miles on the thing to shake it down for the American winter races. I came into the pits a bit white-faced and pink-eyed and they asked me what it was like. What was it like? It wasn't too bad at all, really; there was nothing seriously wrong, it just adopted a slightly nose up attitude – like about 15 degrees to the road surface – at any kind of speed, and with a foot between the front tyres and the tarmac the steering did feel just a *leetle* bit light ..."

Then Chapman started to design the Lotus 40 and once

The Shelby American Cobra Coupé programme

It took a brave man to race a Lotus 30, and an even braver one to power slide it! Jack at Silverstone.
(Jack Sears Archive)

Jack Sears slides the fickle Lotus 30 round Silverstone's Club Corner.
(Jack Sears Archive)

more called on Jack to do some testing of the car, which was notable for having a 5.3 litre Ford V8 engine. "The Lotus 40 was a different kettle of fish altogether. I didn't like the way it handled at all. With the Lotus 30 you could drift it on power but you could not do that with the 40."

By September, Jack Sears' 1965 racing season was virtually over and he began to think about 1966. However, Colin Chapman telephoned him to say that he had organised a test day at Silverstone for the Lotus 40 and he also wanted Jack to do a number of laps in Jim Clark's Indianapolis-winning Lotus. For reasons which has become lost in the mists of time, it was decided to remove the offset suspension on the Indy car and replace it with normal symmetrical suspension, as Jim Clark was going to run it in the European Hill Climb Championship meeting at Ollon Villars in Switzerland. This work had been done and Jim Endruweit, Lotus chief mechanic, was sent to Silverstone with both the Indy car and the Lotus 40.

It was to be a fateful day; says Jack: "On that day in late September, I had the privilege and excitement of driving Jimmy's Indy car at Silverstone. Now, Colin didn't want me to do any fast laps with it, just to make sure the wheels turned properly and the brakes were okay. I was told not to go off and do any fancy laps as that was Jimmy's prerogative.

"That was the fastest car I have ever driven in my life. It was seriously, breathtakingly quick, and I can remember thinking to myself 'If this is what Indianapolis is all about I would have reservations whether I would ever want to do it'. After ten laps or so that was duty number one finished.

"Now Jim Endruweit rolled out the Lotus 40; same day, just a few hours later. We were testing tyres and had sets of Goodyears and Firestones; we got through the morning all right and they had the information they wanted. We then went down to the White Horse in Silverstone village for a sandwich, which was usual when we were testing there, and returned to the circuit after. Off I went again and did several more laps, but coming up through Abbey, the fastest corner on the circuit, I went off. I simply cannot remember the details of spinning but the car slewed across the circuit and turned back, hitting a barrier on the left, overturned, and I woke up in the ambulance on the way to Northampton hospital. Strangely enough, I felt no pain as they had possibly given me some morphine. Jim Endruweit was with me in the ambulance and I asked him what happened. Jim explained

Jennifer Sears, Jack's younger daughter, was another driver of the Atco toy car used by her father. (Jack Sears Archive)

that the car had turned over, trapping me underneath, and they had to lift the car off me. He also told me not to try and move my left arm as it had been nearly severed in the accident. They didn't know that I had cracked a vertebrae in my neck but, thankfully, it had not damaged my spinal cord. I was very lucky.

"My wife, Cicely, arrived from Norfolk, by which time I realised I had a bit of a problem: when the car was upside down either the header tank had split or the cap had come off and scalded me all down my left side, for which I needed a skin graft."

Jack's daughter, Jennifer, was very young and has her own vivid memories. "I remember in the afternoon of that day I kept asking for daddy, and mummy told me he would be home soon. I was only five years old and was having a bath when the telephone rang and mum disappeared to answer it. When she returned I could see she was crying and she told me that daddy had had an accident and she was going to the hospital. I desperately wanted her to take me with her but she said no and that we would see daddy later. Now, of course, I know the whole story but, at that stage, I just knew my dad was very ill. The main thing I remember, however, was a few days later going to the hospital with mum, sitting on the bed and watching *The Magic Roundabout* on children's television." Jack's other daughter, Suzanne, was at boarding school and was taken to the headmistress and told of her father's accident.

Back in hospital, Jack Sears had contracted in infection in his crushed arm and was not allowed to leave until he had recovered. There was a great deal of concern about Jack's arm, and talk of amputation. Jack insisted that he wanted to contact his former surgeon, Ken McKee, to have a look at it, but for this he needed to be transferred across the country to Norwich General Hospital. He spent six weeks in Northampton General before he was released. Cicely drove him to Norwich complete with a plaster cast on his damaged arm.

Mike McKee remembers the occasion. "They wanted to amputate Jack's arm because it was a mess. Jack said that before they did anything he wanted to speak to my father. When he arrived in Norwich, dad said that it would take a long time but he felt he could get Jack's arm working again. He pieced all the bones together with brackets and screws, and I used to go and see Jack most days. He got his wife to ask me to bring more gin and tonic to the hospital."

Working alongside Ken McKee was his specialist plastic surgeon Frank Innes. Jack admired Innes' down-to-earth approach. "I remember the first time I met the plastic surgeon he said 'My name is Frank Innes, I'm in the business of moving skin about the place. I can move skin anywhere'. He said it in such a way it relieved all the tension." The work the pair did together repaired Sears' arm to the extent that he has almost full use of it today, and Innes took skin grafts from all over Jack's body to recreate it. The whole process took an entire year.

"That whole scenario meant that, from September 1965 to the end of 1966, there was no way I could have gone racing. I therefore made the decision to retire from motor racing. Had I continued, as perhaps I could have done in 1967, I would have been in the GT40 programme with Alan Mann, but that's just how the cookie crumbles, sometimes."

Despite all of this, the thirst for excitement never left Jack, and he decided that flying might take the place of motor racing. Happily for Jack, an ideal opportunity was to present itself.

"Sir John Whitmore telephoned me one day to say that he was taking up flying. He had bought a Beech Musketeer and had an ideal landing site in front of his family home, Orsett Hall in Essex. He suggested that I might learn to fly with him as he had this commercial pilot friend who was also a qualified instructor lined up to take him through the course.

"I therefore moved up to Orsett Hall and stayed there for three weeks whilst we took turns in the Beech with the instructor. In that short space of time we not only completed the course but gained our pilot licences. As I didn't own a plane I joined the Norfolk and Norwich Aero Club based at Swanton Morley, and from time to time hired its club plane. As I was a member of the board of the British Racing Drivers Club, and a Director of Silverstone Circuits Ltd, I would occasionally fly to our board meetings and race meetings if the weather was good enough."

The London-Sydney Marathon

Jack Sears returned to full-time farming at Uphall Grange. His family was fast growing up and there was a lot of work to do during his recovery period. However, two of Jack's old friends had something else up their sleeves ...

Tommy Sopwith and Jocelyn Stevens – now Sir Jocelyn Stevens – decided it was time that Britain had a big motor sport event. Jocelyn Stevens became something of an enfant terrible of publishing in the trendy 1960s when he transformed *The Queen* magazine, founded in 1861, into *Queen*. He was born into one of Britain's most famous publishing families, the Hultons, led by patriarch Sir Edward Hulton. Edward Hulton was the founder of *Picture Post* magazine and had extensive holdings in British publishing. On his death, Jocelyn Stevens inherited his fortune but it was *Queen* magazine that made his name, which he and his great friend, photographer Patrick Lichfield, created between them. Later, the magazine was sold to Harpers and became *Harpers & Queen* though, somehow, the spark that Stevens and Lichfield had generated in the magazine was extinguished. Stevens went on to rescue the *London Evening Standard* newspaper after joining Sir Max Aitken at the *Daily Express*. In recent years, he has been Chairman of English Heritage.

As Stevens and Sopwith were great friends of Sir Max Aitken, Chairman of the *Daily Express* Group, they proposed a round-the-world rally. Aitken asked them what they had in mind, so they found a globe of the world and spun it. When it stopped at Australia the idea of a rally from London to Sydney was born. Max Aitken thought the concept was fantastic but explained that he could not afford to sponsor the entire event on *Daily Express* money. His old RAF squadron friend, Australian newspaper tycoon, Sir Frank Packer, came to mind. "We will get Frank to sponsor the Australian section and I will sponsor it to Bombay" he said. Not being one to dally Aitken picked up

Party time during the London-Sydney Marathon. Sir Jocelyn Stephens and Jack have fun whilst Tony Ambrose looks on. (Jack Sears Archive)

THE LONDON-SYDNEY MARATHON

Tommy Sopwith and Jack Sears get planning the London-Sydney Marathon of 1968. (Jack Sears Archive)

the telephone and spoke directly to Frank Packer in Sydney, explaining the idea of a rally from London to Sydney, and asking whether Frank would sponsor the Australian section. Fortunately, Packer also thought it was a wonderful idea and agreed on the spot!

Considering how decisions are usually arrived at in major companies today, it is almost beyond comprehension that, in such a short space of time, two guys should come up with a very rough idea, make a firm decision about what it should actually be, and then have it sponsored by two of the largest newspaper groups in the world. No lawyers, no detailed outlines, no serious costings; just a great promotional idea at a time when newspapers were receptive to large and grand schemes. It simply could not happen like that today. With the backing assured, Tommy Sopwith and Jocelyn Stevens now had to come up with an organisational team as they were clearly unable to work out the sheer logistics of such a massive undertaking on their own.

GENTLEMAN JACK

During the recce for the London-Sydney Marathon the team met some strange traffic on the road ... (Jack Sears Archive)

The Lattaban Pass in Afghanistan was typical of some of the London-Sydney special stages. (Jack Sears Archive)

During the summer of 1967, Jack Sears – now fully recovered from his accident – was working on the farm, and very much involved as a committee member of the British Racing Drivers Club and the RAC Motorsports Association. One day, the phone rang and it was his old friend and former race entrant, Tommy Sopwith, on the line. Tommy asked when Jack could meet him in London as he had a proposition to put to him. Intrigued, but at the same time wary, Jack said he was not sure he wanted to know about any proposition, but agreed to go to London and stay with Tommy in his mews house. When he arrived he was surprised to find there another old friend, Jocelyn Stevens. Jack was offered a drink and then Sopwith got down to business.

As Sears recalls: "There was this big globe of the world on a stand. They said they had spoken to Max Aitken and to Frank Packer of the *Sydney Morning Telegraph*, and there was going to be a rally from London to Sydney, which I was to organise.

"I told them they must be joking, I had a farm to run, to which they replied that as I had stopped motor racing I must have a gap in my life, and it would only take a couple of days a week anyway: surely I could sort it out? Well, I had just sunk my first dry Martini – Tommy mixed a mean dry Martini – when Tommy said 'Have another one'. We went to a fancy restaurant for dinner, both of them terribly enthusiastic about this rally idea, and wouldn't it be fun driving through all those countries? They said I would have to make a reconnaissance of the route to Bombay. All in all, they plied me with a lot of drink and a lot of charm, the long and the short of which was that I agreed to do it and a suitable fee was agreed."

Tommy Sopwith arranged with Max Aitken that Jack Sears should have an office in the *Daily Express* building in Fleet Street, and a secretary – Jane Appleby – who had previously helped Tommy Sopwith organise the various powerboat races he was involved with. Jane was the ideal person to work with as she knew that organising such things never went smoothly, and was aware of some of the potential problems. As it turned out the task was so huge that Jack ended up with three secretaries working on the event.

The original forecast of the job taking two days a week was way off the mark, and Jack was in London all week right from the start, working on the outline of the event and then the logistics. This continued through the autumn of 1967, with Jack staying in a hotel all week and then dashing back to Norfolk and the farm for the weekend.

His farm secretary agreed to come on Saturdays so that they could get through the farming affairs before Jack had to return to London for the Monday morning. By the end of December 1967, Jack realised he could no longer organise this nightmare of an event on his own. He also realised that as he had been out of rallying for seven years, he really needed a rally man to take over that part, and suggested to Tommy Sopwith that the internationally known rally co-driver, Tony Ambrose, would be an ideal person for the job. Max Aitken saw the problem that Jack had and agreed that Tony Ambrose should join the team and, with Jack, do the recces from London to Bombay and from Perth to Sydney.

There was a brief break over Christmas and New Year, although Jack and Tony still had to make final preparations and arrange a multitude of visas so that they could set out on the recce from London to Bombay. They planned this for February 1968, taking with them Michael Wood-Power, who had his own travel business, and even ran an overland bus service to India direct from London. His experience of travel logistics made him the ideal third man.

The world's political situation in 1968 was a lot less fraught than it is today, so it was possible to plan this great adventure to run through such exotic places as Afghanistan, Iran, West Pakistan and India. During the recce there was snow on the road all the way from Turkey to Afghanistan, the route taking them over the infamous Latteban Pass and Khyber Pass into Pakistan, providing a tough test for both man and machine (in this case a Ford Cortina Mark II loaned by Ford). However, this was nothing compared to the amount of red tape that had to be negotiated along the way, with Afghanistan a good example. There were only two roads into Pakistan; the northern route that only four-wheel drive vehicles could negotiate, and the southern route that had been built by the Americans. Obviously, this was the preferred route and permission was eventually granted to use it. Needless to say, a few cases of whisky in the boot of the Cortina helped ease some of the difficult problems faced as well as provide succour for the crew in the extreme cold.

It took Jack and Tony three weeks to complete the recce, as in every country visited they had to go to the capital city and meet with various government departments to ensure the correct permissions were in place, and also assorted motor club delegates to organise the marshals. Says Jack: "Rather than write to them ahead of time we simply turned up with our business cards and sold them on the idea of a rally that would improve tourism in the area, plus national and international newspaper publicity. Generally speaking, this method worked and most of the government officials were extremely helpful. We were usually held up for at least an hour at every border we crossed as they were always questioning things but we could not speak their language and they could not speak ours. We carried four spare wheels on our roof rack for dry weather and a set of studded tyres for the snow. Every night we stopped at a hotel we had to take these tyres off the roof as we knew damn well they would not be there in the morning if we left them. It was a fascinating experience."

In May 1968 it was time to visit Australia and recce the

Michael-Wood Power and Tony Ambrose with the Ford Cortina used for the London-Sydney Marathon recce. (Jack Sears Archive)

route from Perth to Sydney. This was Jack's first meeting with the legendary Packer family. Frank Packer was an ex-RAF fighter pilot who was very much in control of his newspaper, radio and television empire. He had appointed his son, Kerry, company liaison for the event, so it was he who provided everything they needed when in Australia. "Kerry was really helpful, full of fun, and took us out on the town in Sydney. Later, as the years rolled by and the Kerry Packer story unfolded, I was proud to have been involved with him and to see the huge success he had made of the business after his father died."

From Sydney Jack and Tony Ambrose flew to Perth in Western Australia and picked up a BMC 'Land Crab', the rather ungainly 1800cc saloon that BMC was rallying at the time. They were joined by John McKittrick, one of Australia's leading rally competitors, who was familiar with many of the stages that were to be covered on the marathon, along a route of nearly 3500 miles.

Throughout 1968, thanks to the *Daily Express*, the publicity drum was beating hard and strong, and manufacturers took an interest. Apart from hardened professional rally drivers, many amateurs took part and turned up in the strangest cars. One of these was the 8-litre Bentley run by Keith Schellenberg, another power boat racer and adventurer and great friend of Tommy Sopwith, who planned to run with his Scottish racing driver and powerboat fanatic, Norman Barclay. As third man they took along another Scot, who was responsible for developing historic motor racing in Britain, the Honourable Patrick Lindsay. Patrick had already experienced long distance driving when he found a remarkable old Rolls-Royce in India and drove it back to London.

Looking at the schedule today, and the cars of the time, the rally promised a punishing schedule as the crews had to average 1000 miles a day in order to get to Bombay in a week. There were no overnight stops but there was a six hour halt at Kabul in Afghanistan to wait for the Kyber Pass opening at dawn. If the teams could make up time and get any sleep it was to their advantage but, other than Kabul, no rest allowances were worked into the schedule. Average speed was set at 40mph so that on certain sections competitors could make up two or three hours to have a break and a sleep, but the rally continued day and night. Upon arrival in Australia, the marathon ran for another four days and nights from Perth in Western Australia to Sydney.

In the end there were 100 entrants, 98 of which actually started from Crystal Palace. Unbeknown to the competitors, Jack had been told by P&O, the shipping company, that there was space for only 70 cars on the ferry from Bombay to Perth in Australia. As a result everyone on the organisational side was hoping that there would be serious attrition on the way to Bombay. As luck would have it, 72 cars actually reached Bombay, and, with a bit of judicious pushing and shoving, all 72 were squeezed onto the boat. Sadly, it did not include the Schellenberg Bentley which had gone off the road, arriving in Bombay after an epic recovery to find that the boat had sailed. In order to cover all eventualities, the control in Bombay had been open for three days and nights clocking in competitors.

"Imagine having to sit in an office in London knowing you had 100 entries and wondering how many would get to Bombay. Then there were other concerns such as what would happen if the boat left Bombay with only 20 cars onboard? We needed to have a decent entry arrive in Australia to get any publicity at all. Also, the boat was set to leave at a certain time on a certain day, and if there was a huge delay on the way to Bombay we were really in trouble.

"Actually, several competitors arrived late in Bombay to find the boat had departed, so then had to turn round and drive all the way back to London. The logistics of the thing were enormous."

What has never been properly explained is that this particular trip on the SS Chusan from Bombay to Perth in Australia was undertaken by P&O out of a kindness and willingness to help out with the rally. Though the original route had included Bombay, this had been changed, with the route passing Ceylon on the way to Australia. The Chusan was therefore diverted to Bombay simply to transport the cars on the rally. P&O also decided that the first class deck would be kept exclusively for the rally drivers, with other passengers taking the second class deck. However, there was a slight problem with this: second class was full of young Australian girls going home for Christmas. Jack Sears and the organisers felt that one of the rally officials should stay on the boat to try and keep order amongst the competitors whilst the rest flew ahead to Perth to prepare for the Australian landing. The man who drew the short straw was the RAC's senior steward, Jack Kemsley, a highly respected official.

With a smile Jack remembers: "Quite naturally, the rally competitors found the second class deck a bit more interesting than the first class so were in the habit of going downstairs to 'fraternise'. This upset the rhythm of the ship and the Captain, who discussed the matter with Jack Kemsley.

Jack was quite matter-of-fact about the situation and told the Captain that he was not going to intervene, pointing out that they were going to be at sea for ten days, it wasn't possible to stop young people getting togther, and they weren't doing any harm, in any case. Jack suggested that the best thing to do was turn a blind eye to it!

Former BMC and Castrol competitions manager, Stuart Turner, tells of an amusing incident early in the London-Sydney Marathon. As one of the event's official marshals, he was in the company of Jack Sears and a few other notables. "For some reason we stopped off in Nice when travelling to Turkey to marshal. That evening, after dinner, we ended up in a nightclub where a charming coloured hostess joined us at our table. Jack was chatting with her until she got up and left. Then the cabaret started and who should appear on stage but the very same lady. She danced for a bit and then threw her Zeppelin-sized bra into the darkness towards Jack, asking 'You like this, Yack?'. I don't know if Jack liked it or not, I never actually asked him, but it was a wonderful moment. The next morning Jack told us not to tell Tommy Sopwith about the nightclub visit as we had blown a good part of the expenses we had been given for the trip!"

The London-Sydney was a true marathon event that has remained in the memory of all who took part in it. It was won by Scot, Andrew Cowan, co-driver, Colin Malkin, and navigator, Brian Coyle, driving a Hillman Hunter officially entered by Rootes, though very much a low-key affair: so low-key, in fact, that when the marathon ended, Rootes didn't even engage anyone to take any official photographs. Not only was the Hillman Hunter completely standard, it weighed more than a catalogue model because, in the final few days, additional spares kept being added to it. The final straw was a spare radiator mounted inside the boot lid.

As Andrew Cowan's biographer, I obtained a lot of information about the car, some of which the late Des O'Dell, competitions manager for Rootes at the time, asked me not to publish but which I can relate now. In the final run-up to the event Des was concerned about the back axle on the Hillman Hunter, specifically whether it would stand up to the additional weight on the rough roads in Europe and Australia. He then had a brilliant idea and approached his previous employer, Aston Martin, to borrow an Aston Martin back axle for the Hunter!

No-one was more elated after the event than Jack Sears. "The rally turned out to be a huge success and, after the event, I was in my hotel room in Sydney preparing for the celebrations when the phone rang. It was Max Aitken. 'Jack, well done!' he congratulated me; I was really touched that he had taken the trouble to phone because we had sweated blood on the whole thing."

At the end of it all the publicity generated in Britain was such that the Prime Minister of the day, Harold Wilson, sent

Jack Sears. (Jack Sears Archive)

a cabinet minister down to Heathrow to meet the winners on their reurn from Australia.

On his return, Jack had a lot of catching up to do at the farm but had more time to devote to his family. He maintained his links with motor sport, however, by chairing a number of committees in the RAC, as well as his work with the British Racing Drivers Club.

During this period Jack's son, David, was becoming more and more interested in motor sport and, as detailed in the next chapter, did develop a career in racing, even though Jack gave him little or no encouragement. This, presumably, was for the obvious reason that although Jack knew that the sport provided many highs, he was all too aware of the lows and the ever-present risk of accident that it also entailed. Despite, this, he was very proud of David's achievements.

Some time later, in 1992, Jack Sears was elected President of the BRDC, of which he had been a member for 38 years. For Jack it was a crowning moment and a satisfying accolade and acknowledgement of the time and effort he had put into his years on the board. His roles within the RAC, which had included Chairman of the RAC Race Committee, had been rewarding in their own way, but to be elected President of the club he loved was a great pleasure for him. However, circumstances were also to make it something of a poisoned chalice as the BRDC was about to face the first serious crisis in its long and notable history.

With its considerable holdings, notably the land around Silvestone circuit, the British Racing Drivers Club comprised various separate companies, including Silverstone Circuits Ltd, the main financial cornerstone of the BRDC. Generally speaking, the members of the board of Silvestone Circuits Ltd derived from the main board of the BRDC, and the man appointed Chairman of Silverstone Circuits Ltd was Tom Walkinshaw.

Tom had come from relatively humble beginnings as a market gardener in Scotland, and had not only become a successful racing driver but also a very successful businessman and wheeler-dealer within motor racing. He also formed and successfully grew Tom Walkinshaw Racing, giving Jaguar and Rover championships in touring cars. Tom then moved into Formula One, first in partnership with Flavio Briatore at Benetton, and then as owner of the Arrows Formula One team. At the time, the early 1990s, he was on top of the world, a clear asset to Silverstone Circuits Ltd.

Silverstone Circuits Ltd was cash-rich and Tom Walkinshaw saw this as an opportunity for the company to diversify, and proposed a joint venture between his TWR garage group and Silverstone Circuits Ltd to develop the motor business. Though the motor trade was going through one of its periodic sales downturns, Walkinshaw felt that this was a temporary blip, and that when new sales revived in a few years' time, the joint venture could be sold for a considerable profit.

This proposal passed through the correct channels, including the board of Silverstone Circuits Ltd and the board of the BRDC though, with hindsight, it is apparent that it would not meet with the approval of the BRDC membership. The club included more than a few members in the motor trade who would have welcomed such a deal between Silverstone Circuts Ltd and their own garages. This was the start of a bitter struggle within the club, elements of which reverberate to this day.

Jack Sears, the new President of the BRDC, was faced with something of a revolution which led, as he admits today, to probably the saddest and most traumatic period of his

The London-Sydney Marathon

Jack Sears' Ferrari GTO parked outside his house. The car now resides in the United States of America. (Jack Sears Archive)

well-ordered life. Despite his success, or because of it, Tom Walkinshaw had ruffled many feathers on his way up the motor racing ladder; he has that ruthless and determined streak that often brings success, particularly in the tough business of motor racing, so did not have to look very far to find enemies. The whole affair plunged the club into turmoil with various factions taking stands as more and more information emerged about the proposed deal. In the end, it was voted down by the membership and in the aftermath Jack Sears and the board stepped down and a new board was elected with Innes Ireland nominated President of the Club. In light of his helter-skelter career in motor racing, Innes Ireland may not have seemed the ideal choice, but it transformed him and he did a major job in stamping his authority pulling together the various factions that existed within the club. Tragically it was a short-lived period as Innes was already suffering from terminal cancer, and within two years had died. For Jack Sears this was a period of great sadness and distress, which he is reluctant to discuss even today ...

Late in 1968 Jack and Cicely Sears, with their former rally driving friend, the late Dennis Scott, had been deerstalking in the West Highlands of Scotland on Cameron of Locheil's estate. On the way home Jack and Cicely called in to see Neil and Freda Corner in Durham because Jack was keen to see the old GTO he had raced. Neil let Jack have a drive in the car, and once more he was absolutely captivated. Jack suggested to Neil that if he ever wished to sell the car to let him know and give him the first offer. Two years later, in 1970, Neil Corner bought some of Stanley Sears' cars – the 1901 Mors, the 1914 TT Sunbeam, and the 1914 Grand Prix Opel – and mentioned that he now had a 1964-bodied GTO that he wanted to keep. He offered to sell Jack Sears the

107

GENTLEMAN JACK

Jack with his present wife, Diana. (Jack Sears Archive)

ex-Coombs GTO which became part of the Sears household, where it remained for twenty-nine years.

In 1995 Jack Sears lost his wife, Cicely, to a heart attack after forty-two years of marriage. Jack was totally devastated as Cicely had enthusiastically supported him throughout his racing, sharing events like the London-Brighton run and attending countless social functions. She was also devoted to their three children and saw them through the tough teenage years. Jack, Cicely and the children used to go on holiday together with another couple, Raymond and Diana Woolf, and their family. Diana was Cicely's best friend. Raymond died of cancer in 1990 and after Cicely's death Jack and Diana used to team up to attend various social functions. They fell in love and married in 1997. As Jack explained, he and Diana had no secrets as the families had known each other for so long. Because of this Diana has become a second mother to Jack's children and Jack a father figure to Diana's two daughters. Diana, too, is keen on motor sport and attends most of the events with Jack.

As a Ferrari owner Jack was a prominent member of the Ferrari Owners Club, and often took his GTO to club events. John Anderson, then Chairman of the FOC, invited Jack to a function where he explained that he was nearing the end of his two stints as Chairman of the Club, and would Jack like to succeed him? Jack asked for time to think about this as he had only recently married Diana, and was not sure whether she would approve of him taking on further motor sport responsibilities. As it turned out Diana was very much in favour of the idea so Jack accepted and in 2000 became Chairman of the Ferrari Owners Club.

As usual Jack threw himself into the task, and has been a diligent Chairman, attending countless events all over Britain and generally waving the Ferrari Owners Club flag. The Club has a racing championship, a hill climb championship, a superb concours d'elegance, and various social functions. In 2006, after his two three-year terms, Jack was asked to stay on as Chairman until April 2008.

Jack's son, David, developed his own successful career in motor racing, and his daughters have also maintained links with the sport. Jennifer was David's personal assistant for some time and their sister, Suzanne, works with the auctioneer, Bonhams, and has also begun to dabble in motor racing by taking part in the 2006 Formula Woman competition to find new British woman racing drivers. Unfortunately, in the tests to choose the finalists at Bruntingthorpe, Suzanne was eliminated, although her licence has not gone to waste as she has been racing the Morgan of her partner, James Paterson.

Jack Sears is just as busy today as he has always been, attending to the farm which, like everything to do with Jack, is as immaculate and tidy as a farm could hope to be. His day-to-day farm transport is a trusty Mitsubishi Shogun 4x4. Now 78, Jack has led a remarkable life both in and out of cars, and personifies the private entrant enthusiast who is willing to drive anything, be it a racing car or a rally car. Part of his life are the many souvenirs, trophies, photographs and cuttings he has gathered, as well as all his memories. Along with Diana, he positively basks in the warmth and friendship of people he has never previously met but who chat to him about his racing. Few people in racing have achieved such a peaceful and contented retirement ...

Following in father's footsteps; Jack Sears' daughters, Suzanne (left) and Jennifer, with Jack on a racing school course. (Jack Sears Archive)

David Sears – Entrepreneur

Even a short conversation with David Sears reveals his dogged determination to succeed in everything he does. Beneath that friendly and affable exterior lies a hard-hitting businessman whose influence on the motor racing scene is far greater than a cursory glance at his career might indicate.

Though his grandfather and father drifted away from what could be called mainstream industry and moved into farming, there is little doubt that David has inherited the genes of his great-grandfather, founder of the original Sears shoe empire. Like him, David has developed his present career almost entirely on his own; Jack Sears may probably have preferred him to become a farmer and, perhaps, semi-professional racing driver, but farming was not for David.

David Sears was born at Uphall Grange on December 9 1955, just before his father was due to drive in the Monte Carlo Rally with Archie Scott Brown. Archie and *Autocar* Sports Editor, Peter Garnier, became David's godfathers.

He began to display his commercial talents early in life. His sisters recall the occasion when the three family pet rabbits, Flopsy, Mopsy and Cotton Tail, were taken by David to Downham Market and sold to buy parts for his bicycle. When his sisters complained about this, and enquired about their share of the money, David commented that he was the one who had taken the rabbits and sold them so the money was his! The children had an engineless go-kart that was towed behind a tractor; an engine was added but, one day, the kart disappeared. It had been sold by David to help him finance a motor bike.

As Suzanne recalls "David was very clever with his buying

David Sears. (Courtesy Sutton Photographics)

David Sears — entrepreneur

and selling. He would buy motor bikes, tweak them, and then sell them for a profit in order to save up for his first car. He always seemed to buy flash cars. He used these same skills to save up to do the Jim Russell School."

It is interesting that, throughout his racing career, David Sears received no financial help from his father; Jack did not want to feel responsible if he financed David's racing and then David had an accident. On one occasion, however, Jack did loan David some of the money to finance his first Formula 3 car but, as David points out, the loan was paid back with interest.

David Sears, then, has carved out his own career on his own terms and has been extremely successful. As was mentioned in Jack Sears' biography, he learned to drive in a little Atco-powered car that was kept in the family until David reached an age when he could take it over. "When I was a little boy my first motorised transport was this Atco trainer on which my father learned to drive in 1938. In fact, we are restoring this little car to original condition at the moment for a future generation to enjoy.

"Then there was the go-kart we built up. I actually wanted to start kart racing but my father didn't think it was a very good idea. When I was seventeen I secretly booked myself into the Jim Russell Racing School at Snetterton and did a course, but no racing as I couldn't afford it. I did it in bits and pieces at a time but, inevitably, ran out of money. I went to John

Portent of things to come. A promotional photo of Jack Sears with young son, David, and battery-powered miniature Lotus. (Jack Sears Archive)

111

Second generation. Jack Sears explains the controls of the Atco Trainer, powered by a lawnmower engine, to son and future racing driver, David Sears. The car was originally given to Jack and his brother, Eric, by their grandmother. (Jack Sears Archive)

Kirkpatrick, who was running the course, to explain that I didn't have the money to continue. As the result of a party joke, I had a pierced ear in which I wore an earring. John looked at this and, in his broad Scottish accent, said: "Real racing drivers don't wear earrings, take that bloody thing out." Later, I received a phone call from Jim Russell who offered me the chance to continue the course and do a couple of races to see how I got on. In the end I was given two races, one at Snetterton and one at Silverstone, and won them both."

By this time David was working on the farm with his father as he had left his school, Charterhouse, a year into his A-levels because he didn't like the idea of a single-sex school, nor the rigid discipline it implied. Instead, he went to technical college and did a business course.

David had obviously attended a number of motor racing meetings when his father was racing, and was brought up in a household where many famous racing drivers came and went regularly. He has no doubt who his favourite was: "For me, Jimmy Clark was the nicest man and the best driver. In fact, he and Ayrton Senna are to me the finest natural talents we have ever seen in motor racing."

However, now with two school wins under his belt, David was even more determined to get into motor racing. He persuaded an old school friend, Nick Dixon, a member of the family which produced Dixcel toilet paper and bathroom tissue, to invest some of his inheritance in David's racing career. "The Dixon family was really kind to me. Nick helped me and paid for all my mistakes in the first three years until, finally, I got a works deal with Royale. Those Royales were designed by Rory Byrne, who went on to design the Schumacher Ferraris."

David's first season in racing followed a very common pattern of inferior cars and lack of money. He started out with a Van Diemen and found himself racing against another newcomer, Nigel Mansell, who was racing the John Lipman-designed Javelin JL5; they had some good races together. After the Van Diemen's suspension collapsed at Oulton Park, David built up a four-year old Crossle 25F, and, to his surprise, put it on the front row of the grid at Thruxton. However, as his sponsorship ran out in June that year, this brought his racing to an end.

His breakthrough came in 1978 when he got his hands on a Royale RP24 and took it to third overall in the British Formula Ford Championship; the highest-placed private entrant that year. That same year David also helped Ralph Firman with the development of the Van Diemen Formula Ford, in order to earn a few pounds, at the same time becoming something of a scout for Ralph by looking out for new driving talent. Little did he realise but this activity was to form part of the foundation of his present success in the motor racing business ...

As a result of his success as a privateer David was approached by Royale and offered a works car on loan for the 1979 racing season. At the same time Minister, a concern at the height of its fame as a Formula Ford engine specialist, offered him works engines. Thus equipped, he realised he was in a position to win championships and entered for both the RAC Formula Ford and P & O Ferries Championships. Rushen Green Racing prepared the car and he was on his way.

The Royale was one of the first racing cars designed by Rory Byrne, who had arrived from Pretoria in South Africa in

Gentleman Jack

1973 to help a friend who was racing one of the original Royales. Byrne's work on his friend's RP16 was so successful that he was offered the job of chief designer for Royale, and later went on to develop a Formula Ford 2000 which gave Toleman Motorsport its start (he joined Toleman to design its own Formula Two car in 1980). When Brian Henton and Derek Warwick finished first and second with the TG280 in the European Formula 2 Championship, Toleman decided to go the whole hog and come into Formula 1 with the TG81 and young Ayrton Senna as driver. From then on, Rory Byrne became one of the most successful Grand Prix car designers, and was instrumental in creating the cars that launched Ferrari's resurgence in the early 2000s.

In 1979 David formed David Sears Motorsport, as even then he could see the potential in running and developing his own team. He shrewdly realised that if multi-talented people were employed they could act as chief mechanic or team manager. In addition, David was still developing his own racing career; the first example of his ability to keep three or four balls in the air at the same time.

For David, that season was a true baptism of fire; as a 'works' driver he secured two British Formula Ford Championships with nineteen wins and seven seconds. His double championship-winning Royale was prepared for him by Pat Symonds, who also prepared the 2005 and 2006 world championship-winning Renaults for Fernando Alonso. It was also his first introduction to European circuits. Moving into Europe not only brought a new challenge but also opened his eyes to the more laidback attitude of European culture, where the food and ambience were totally different to what he had been used to, and gave him more experience to pass on to the drivers he was beginning to run in his own team.

David Sears Motorsport's first driver was Cal Foster, son of the famous architect, Sir Norman Foster (now Lord Foster

Donington 1959, David Leslie, left, and David Sears, who drove the factory Aston Martin AML1. (Author collection)

of Thames Bank). Sadly, Cal later fell out with his father and was forced to stop racing. At the end of the 1979 season David had won one of the Grovewood Awards for the most promising British and Commonwealth driver of the year.

But what did his father, Jack Sears, make of all this?

"He didn't think it was all a good idea for, in his words, he felt that he had broken several bones in his body and his neck which eventually caused him to stop racing. So he didn't feel that paying for his son to go racing was right when a similar thing could happen. I tried to convince him that cars were safer in my day than they were in his, but he was having none of it and told me that if I wanted to make my way as a racing driver I would have to do it myself.

"After I had won the 1979 Formula Ford Championships and been the so-called star of the Formula Ford Festival, even though I did not actually win it, I was called by Colin Chapman to test a Lotus Formula 1 car at Paul Ricard. I got to the end of the season, and my then girlfriend – later my wife and mother of my son, John – took me to Kenya for a holiday. I was excited at the prospect of testing the Lotus when I got back in December but, due to bad weather forecasts in early December, Colin brought the test forward to late November. There weren't mobile phones then, and nobody could contact me. Colin rang my dad to ask where I was and dad told him I was in Kenya; sadly, that was it. Colin never asked you a second time and Roberto Moreno got the testing contract."

It was logical that David's next move should be into Formula 3, with support from Rushen Green. Initially, there was talk of a factory March but, at the end of the day, Jo Marquart offered an Argo chassis backed by Glover Oil and Circuit Travel, together with the factory cars of Roberto Guerrero and Thierry Tassin. That same season he ran in the BMW County Championship and won the series, driving alongside the likes of Martin Brundle and Patrick Neve in BMW 323is.

By now David Sears wanted to develop his career in motor racing, not only as a driver but in driver management. His first contracted drivers were Alan Menu and Pedro Chaves with Formula Fords. Then there was hopeful, Taki Inoue, who had great ambitions to be the new Japanese racing star. He had begun racing in the Japanese Freshman Championship for Touring Cars but realised that, to get on internationally, he had to come to England; David Sears Motorsport was his chosen team.

Takachio (Taki) Inoue was born in Kobe, Japan, and on arrival in Britain enrolled at the Jim Russell Racing School. He was then taken under the corporate wing of David Sears Motorsport for the 1980 racing season, with a Van Diemen. Taki was brave but also accident prone, as David learnt the hard way. Early in the racing season he had a major accident. "Taki had a huge crash at Snetterton in his Formula Ford Van Diemen RF79 and passed out. The medical unit was quick on the scene, kick-started him and carted him off to hospital.

"I went with him in the ambulance, thinking, my God, I've just started the team and one of my drivers has died; what is going to happen? However, Taki woke up in hospital, saw two blonde nurses and me, and burst into tears! Through his tears he said: 'My machine is bloken, bloken.' I told him not to worry about that but to worry about himself."

Inoue wanted to continue racing and, as David had just divorced and was living on his own, he came up with the ideal solution. He suggested that Taki could come and work in the house and do the garden, and his girlfriend could cook and clean, in return for which David would repair the Van Diemen and Taki could race for the rest of the season. "He thought I was some kind of God-like figure at that point. He finished the year and was thrown out of the country as he didn't have a work permit. Gillian Shephard, who later became Minister of Education, was our local MP, and I pleaded with her to help. I had three guys, a new team and company, and needed to get this guy back in 1981. She got him back just before the first race at Silverstone, which saved the day."

Taki Inoue had a chequered racing career, even though he did not shine. He returned to Japan and raced in Formula 3 with a Dallara, but came back to Europe to join up with David Sears once more.

As for David's own racing career, he didn't have the budget to launch into Formula 3 in 1982. However, Irishman, Eddie Jordan, had retired from racing at the end of 1980 and decided to set up his own Formula 3 team using a new Ralt-Toyota. Eddie telephoned David and offered him a drive in the hope that it would help him pick up some sponsorship. At Thruxton he was half a second quicker than the favourite, Jonathan Palmer. In the race, Palmer squeezed through and Sears finished second but lost his drive as Eddie Jordan was still looking for sponsorship.

David did get a drive in the Willhire 24 hour saloon race at Snetterton driving a Ford Capri with Gerry Marshall, and the pair took a strong second place. He also had a few races in the Thundersports series with a Sports 2000 and achieved some good results.

Throughout the 1980, David continued to develop his team though his own driving career progressed in stops and starts. For example, in 1984, Tom Walkinshaw invited David to join the TWR Jaguar XJS team to replace Martin Brundle, and he achieved his greatest success in the Silverstone Tourist Trophy race when he finished second overall.

This period was probably the most important and life-changing part of David Sears' career. He was spending most of his time building up his team, arranging sponsorship with drivers, and generally buckling down to create the foundations of his future outside of motor racing. When a racing opportunity arose, he took it as it provided income to help fund development of his team. Even in 1986 David was helping Ralph Firman develop and test the latest Van Diemen Formula Fords "Just to earn some money. I realised my career was coming to a close and I honestly didn't want to go farming with my dad because I would just be the boy on the farm. I basically decided I did not know anything else I could do that would recreate the excitement and adrenalin racing does, and also provide an income."

All of his networking was beginning to pay off, however, as he was given the chance to race in the IMSA series in the United States, thanks to Chip Ganassi. "Chip was beginning to find that the Indycar cockpit was becoming a bit too tight for him. He was concerned that here was this Englishman (me) who kept going quicker than him. He stopped racing himself and since then we have worked together as I have been able to feed him some good drivers."

David raced a Spice-Pontiac in the Camel Lights series for Ganassi but wanted to concentrate on his own team and driver management business. However, in 1988 he raced an Ecosse Group C2 car with Don Shead in the British Sports Car Championship, and in 1989 was signed to drive for the Aston Martin team at Donington in the World Sports Car Championship event, plus a full contract for the 1990 season. However, on January 1 1990, the Aston Martin effort was scrapped as new owner, Ford, did not want to run both Jaguar and Aston Martin teams in the same championship. One of David's great friends from Formula 3 days, David Kennedy, telephoned to say he was on the lookout for drivers

David Sears with the Aston Martin AMR1 at Donington. (Author collection)

to race for a Japanese team at Le Mans. Kennedy and Tiff Needell chose David Sears and Anthony Reid to share a Porsche 962C sponsored by Alpha, one of Japan's largest building companies. David was looking forward to the race but, shortly before it, broke his elbow in an accident. Despite this, and still bandaged, he ran in the event and the two finished not only third overall behind the TWR XJR12 Jaguars, but as the highest placed private entrants.

It was clear by now that his racing days were over. Earlier in the year he had driven a Porsche 962 in Japan with Will Hoy. At Fuji he crashed and wrecked the car. "The cars cost about £400,000 each and we did about £250,000 worth of damage. I then thought it was about time I stopped, and decided it was time to move on to something else. I was in my mid-thirties, had produced two more children, and decided that running a race team was ten times more difficult than driving a race car."

Sears' success as an entrant and manager certainly took him to a new level and the 1990s saw his team not only win races but also championships. He embraced the Formula Vauxhall Class and won the British Championship with Vincenso Sospiri; Sospiri also finishing second in the European Championship behind Rubens Barrichello.

David Sears moved into serious racing driver management when he signed up a young Swedish driver called Jan Magnussen. He helped Magnussen when he joined Paul Stewart Racing to race in Formula 3, and led him into Formula 1 with the Stewart Grand Prix team.

The next major development in his life occurred in 1993, all within the space of a few weeks, and taxed his formidable organisational skills to the limit. Up until that point David Sears Motorsport operated out of two units at Snetterton but now it was time to develop. David had opened negotiations with Jo Marquart – who designed and developed the Modus and Argo racing cars – to buy the Argo business and premises. "I went on holiday to the Caribbean and Jo Marquart died. On my return his widow telephoned and asked if I was still interested. Meanwhile, I had just negotiated a project with Ying Fa Yoong and Tommy Suharto in Malaysia to create a new concern called Formula Asia and sell cars throughout China and Asia. Then, we had the Formula 3000 project coming onstream, and Teddy Pilette and Count Van De Stratten wanted me to do a Formula 3 project, so I had a load of things on my plate. I thought two's company but three's a crowd and I dropped the Pilette project."

So now David Sears owned the Argo factory and engaged Keith Lane to design the chassis of the Formula Asia car that was launched in 1994. Ultimately, David Sears built around 52 Formula Asia cars and was a manufacturer in his own right. One of the first Formula Asia drivers was Alex Yoong, Ying Fa Yoong's son, who was the rising new star in Malaysia at that time.

Then there was SuperNova racing which has become a large enterprise in itself. This started out as a Formula 3000 project sponsored by Nova, the largest group of language schools in Japan with around 12,000 teachers in outlets all over the country. This developed into the most successful team in the history of Formula 3000, with more race wins and championships than any other team. "I go to Japan two or three times a year and they have been perfect partners," says David.

David's ability to pick out talent was truly paying off. He won the F3000 Championship in 1995 with Vincenzo Sospiri and the 1997 Championship with Riccardo Zonta. Then came his first real star driver contract with a young Colombian that David had first seen racing in karts, by the name of Juan Pablo Montoya. "Juan Pablo and his dad came along at the end of 1997 and asked if we could help him. At the time he had been racing for Helmut Marko who, along with Gerhard Berger, wanted to sign him up on a management contract. However, Juan and I agreed a deal at Jerez when Jacques Villeneuve won the World Championship. As soon as Marko heard about it he threw Juan Pablo and his dad out of the hospitality bus and they came and ate with us. That is why I will never be allowed to run a Red Bull driver in my team as Marko runs the Red Bull affair."

Montoya had only a third of the budget necessary to race in F3000 in 1998, so David managed to secure another third from Japanese sponsors and the rest from Frank Williams, as David was running the Williams Junior team in F3000. He also persuaded Frank Williams to sign Montoya on a test contract. That year, Juan Pablo Montoya gave David Sears his third Formula 3000 Championship victory and things looked good for Montoya to sign for Williams in 2000. However, Frank Williams overlooked Montoya and signed Jenson Button so David took Juan Pablo to the USA. He met up with Chip Ganassi who signed Montoya for CART. Juan won the championship and the Indianapolis 500.

David Sears claimed two more F3000 Championships with Bruno Junquera in 2000 and Frenchman, Sebastien Bourdais, in 2002. Along the way he lost his management role of Juan Pablo Montoya to another manager, but signed up Sebanstien Bourdais who, so far, has given him three successive wins in the CART Championship in 2004, 2005, 2006 and 2007.

Today, David runs two of the leading teams in GP2, which took over from F3000 as the Grand Prix support series, and two teams in the A1 GP Championship. "I would say that, of the teams outside Formula 1, we have been the most profitable over the years. It was not done as a hobby but as a proper business, and we have always had proper sponsorship from the word go." In many ways David Sears has the potential to exert considerable influence over the future direction of motor racing. He is opinionated, and clearly thinks ahead:

David Sears hands over the Aston Martin AMR1 at Donington in 1989. On the right, team manager, Richard Williams, oversees. (Author collection)

The Japanese Alpha Porsche team celebrates after finishing third at Le Mans with Anthony Reid and Tiff Needell (left). (Courtesy Sutton Photographics)

David Sears first saw Juan Pablo Montoya karting as a little boy in Columbia. He later managed Montoya when the Columbian first arrived in Europe. Sears is seen with Montoya after winning the Formula 3000 Championship. (Courtesy Sutton Photographics)

Amongst the drivers David Sears signed to a management contract was Frenchman Sebastien Bourdais, multiple winner of the CART Championship in the United States. Bourdais, left with David Sears. (Jack Sears Archive)

"What I find really difficult is the fact that so many other sports plough money back in and none of the Formula 1 hierarchy, from Bernie downward, put any money back into the grass roots of the sport at all. If they were a bit patriotic all of them could contribute something; but they don't.

"I am training my son, John, at the moment. I thought he was going to be a banker in the City so I suggested to him that he could come in and slowly take over the reins of the race team. I don't want to be running around the world all the time and I want to back off a bit."

Though Jack and David Sears may be as different as chalk and cheese in their attitude toward motor racing, we must not forget that in the fifty years covering their involvement an awful lot has changed. Unfortunately, there is no room in motor racing today for the gentlemanly way of racing that Jack Sears epitomised.

Appendix 1
Stanley Sears and his Collection

Stanley Sears was born in 1903 at a time when his father, John George Sears, had gone from apprentice cobbler to successful businessman in the shoe manufacturing trade in Northampton. He was brought up in relative luxury in the family home, Collingtree Grange.

Even when he was a little boy Stanley loved cars, and spent a lot of his time helping the chauffeur clean and polish the family cars. A great treat was to sit on the chauffeur's lap whilst he was driving, and eventually driving the cars himself in the grounds of the house. This fascination for cars stayed with Stanley all his life, and his passion for old cars meant that he rescued many that might otherwise have been scrapped during the Second World War.

When he went up to Cambridge University, Stanley joined the Cambridge University Motor Club, running his Alvis Silver Eagle in a number of club events, as well as racing it at Brooklands. However, his racing career was short-lived as his mother – by now a young widow – felt that this pastime was much too dangerous for her son, and sternly informed him that she wanted him to stop racing. However, he did compete in rallies still, and, with various Bentleys, was a regular competitor in the RAC Rally during the 1930s. One year he entered the family Phantom III Rolls-Royce, which led to *Autocar's* cartoonist sketching Stanley in action on one of the tests in the lumbering car.

In 1936, Stanley Sears left the shoe business and bought a farm in Bolney, Sussex, which just happened to back onto the route of the London to Brighton Veteran Car Run. Like Mr Toad of Toad Hall, Stanley was fascinated by the veterans as they chuffed past the farm on their way to Brighton, and this encouraged him to begin collecting veteran cars. The Clement Talbot was a particular favourite as it had a four-cylinder rather than a two-cylinder engine, and shaft drive as opposed to chains. The other veteran, the 1901 Mors, stayed in the Sears collection into World War II, but with war came a problem for Stanley Sears.

The Government announced a scrap metal drive to turn scrap steel into armaments, which obviously threatened the countless number of old cars lying around that could not be used during the war due to petrol rationing. The main threat was to some of the old and outdated family cars that were still about but, clearly, this ruling would also affect some of the truly classic cars that had been built over the years and lovingly maintained by private collectors.

Fundamentally, anything that did not run was commandeered and turned into scrap metal. Stanley was worried about his own cars, particularly the Mors (which had been bought to replace the Darracq that had been sold), and the Clement Talbot, both of which were in pristine condition. As Jack Sears recalls: "In fairness to the Government, it was junk metal it was trying to get hold of and not decent cars. My father heard of various nice, collectable cars that were ripe for restoration, and vowed to try and save them.

"He bought anything he could see that was of interest, and had the space in various buildings on the farm in which to store these cars. I cannot remember exactly how many he had at the end of the war but it could have been as many as forty.

"After the war he kept some cars and sold off the rest. He didn't try and profit from this but sold them through the Veteran Car Club, as a lot of veterans were involved. Mind you, he was not alone in doing this as a number of VCC members, who had the space, did the same and an

121

Stanley Sears at the wheel of the 1905 20hp TT Replica Rolls-Royce. (Jack Sears Archive)

Stanley Sears and his wife, Lilian, arrive safely at Brighton with the 1901 Mors. (Jack Sears Archive)

Acquisition Committee was formed on which my father was Chairman.

"It was only after the war that my father built up his personal collection, majoring on Rolls-Royce, which was not surprising as he had a life-long admiration for the cars from Crewe."

After the war Stanley Sears competed in a number of VCC events and became a member of the Committee before being elected President in 1962. Meanwhile, he had acquired one of the best known Bentley specials, the Forrest Lycett 8 litre. Stanley Sears and Forrest Lycett were great friends and knew the entire history of the car. It was originally bought by Lycett in December 1931, sporting an open four-seater Corsica body which he later changed for a two-seater racing body, painted black with maroon mudguards. In their conversations, Stanley Sears often said that if Lycett ever wanted to sell the car he would be interested in buying it. As it turned out, Lycett adjusted his will and instructed his executors that, in the event of his death, Stanley should be contacted and offered the first chance to buy the Bentley.

During 1958, Jack's mother, Lilian, died, leaving Stanley Sears on his own at Bolney. Two years later Stanley married his late wife's best friend, Hester, though, five years later, she was killed in a car accident and Stanley was widowed for the second time. A year later he decided to retire to Bermuda but, deciding that he was too far away from his family, returned after a few years to buy a house in the Portuguese Algarve. Whilst there he met his third wife, Doreen. (After Stanley died in 1988, Doreen returned to England and now lives in London.)

Early in 1960, Forrest Lycett was knocked down and killed by a London taxi, and, as instructed, his executors approached Stanley Sears, who bought the car. When it arrived it needed repainting, and the engine required some attention. L C McKenzie, who had originally prepared the 8 litre engine for Lycett, was contacted, and he and his son completed the rebuild.

Another famous Bentley in the Sears collection was the 1929 supercharged, 4.5 litre which was built by Tim Birkin and financed by Dorothy Paget. An interesting fact is that Dorothy Paget's nephew was Sir Gawaine Baillie, who

Jack Sears chauffeurs his father, Stanley, round Snetterton in the Forrest Lycett 8 litre Bentley. (Jack Sears Archive)

raced alongside and against Jack Sears during his racing career.

Stanley Sears took the car to a new autoroute near Antwerp in the 1960s where the Belgian Automobile Club had permission to hold a speed trial before the road was officially opened to the public. The Lycett 8 litre was clocked at 141mph, a remarkable achievement, and the Birkin car was timed at 126mph, the fastest of the blower Bentleys present.

Occasionaly, Stanley and Jack would compete against each other, and Jack always felt he learned a lot from his father "By and large I was reasonably kind to a car. Any of the mechanics I raced with would tell you this. My father was also kind to his cars. Being an engineer he had a great feel for cars. I can remember him at the Brighton Speed Trials leaving the line in the Bentley, and when it came my turn to drive it I don't think I made as good a start as him. He just seemed to zip away whilst I was slightly hesitant, which was why he beat me on that occasion. He obviously knew the car better than I did and fed the power in smoothly, but he was thrilled to bits to have beaten me."

Later, Stanley Sears commissioned the production of a small, ring binder booklet detailing the cars in his collection. He appointed Thomas Photos in Oxford to photograph the cars, and added the specifications and his comments about each car's background. The only car in his collection that was not photographed was his 1905 6-cylinder Rolls-Royce, and a later photograph has been included in the following reproduction of the information and photographs in this booklet.

A Collection of Interesting Cars
By Stanley E Sears
Bolney, Sussex,
England

Gentleman Jack

The oldest car in Stanley Sears' collection was this 2.4 litre 1901 Mors, purchased in Paris in 1937. (Jack Sears Archive)

1901 Mors

This car was owned by Monsieur R Fernand of Chaumont near Nancy, France, and used by him for many years. When a more modern car was purchased, the Mors was stored in his garage under good conditions until his death, when it was acquired by his son who sold it to a dealer, from whom it was purchased by S E Sears in Paris in 1937, imported to England and restored.

The car stayed in the family until 1970 when it was sold to Neil Corner. Later, it was sold to the RAC and given the registration number 1 RAC. It is now used by the Chairman of the RAC on the London-Brighton run.

Modifications: ... High tension magneto replacing the original low tension type
Engine: ... 4 cylinders, air cooled cylinder barrels and heads, with a belt of water cooling round the inlet and exhaust valves. Automatic inlet valves. Bore: 80mm. Stroke: 120mm. 2410cc. 15.9hp.
Wheelbase: ... 6ft 11½in. Track: 4 feet 4½in
Maximum speed: ... 45mph
Coachbuilder: ... Henry Binder of Paris

126

1903 Clement Talbot

Originally owned by Lord Drew of Wadhurst Hall, Surrey until 1920, when it was purchased by S Upton of Holmshill Farm, Chiddingly, Sussex, who used it regularly until 1924. It was then sold to Roy Whitelea, and was acquired by S E Sears in 1936 and completely restored.

Modifications: ... ... Zenith carburettor fitted in about 1911 in place of the original Languemare
Engine: ... ... 4 cylinder side valve. Bore: 85mm. Stroke: 120mm. 2720cc. i8hp
Wheelbase: ... ... 7ft 5in. Track: 4ft 4½in
Weight: ... ... 19cwt 1 quarter
Tyres: ... ... 875x105 = 35½in diameter
Maximum speed: 40mph
Coachbuilder: ... ... Rothschild et Fils – Paris

This 1903 Clement-Talbot was a cornerstone of Stanley Sears' collection. (Jack Sears Archive)

Gentleman Jack

The Stanley Sears 4 litre 1904 Mercedes. (Jack Sears Archive)

1904 Mercedes

The car was successfully raced by Tom Faulkner at Brooklands during the period 1906-1908: restored by C R Abbott in 1947 and won many awards in VCC events. Purchased by S E Sears in July, 1950.

Modifications: . ... .Zenith carburettor in place of Mercedes type
Engine:.... .... .4 cylinder, T head. Bore: 100mm. Stroke 130mm. 4028cc. 24.8hp
Wheelbase:. .... .7ft 11½in. Track: 4ft 4in
Weight: 18¾cwt
Maximum speed:. 65-70mph
Coachbuilder:. .... .Replica of the original 2-seater racing type built by C R Abbott

1905 Rolls-Royce 20hp

This car was reconstructed from two identical chassis: no 40520 found in Cornwall and no 26350 found at Brae Cottage, Knutsford, where Sir Henry Royce lived for many years. Both chassis had many missing or damaged parts, and the complete car utilises parts from the two. Stanley Sears wanted to put a replica body on it identical to that of the car which finished in second place in the first Tourist Trophy race and that Charles Rolls won the second TT with the following year, 1906. As he was very friendly with the board of Rolls-Royce, Sears was able to obtain the original factory drawings of the bodywork and the replica was produced by Harringtons.

Modifications:	The Zenith carburettor is not original. The Rolls-Royce carburettor was missing from both of the chassis
Engine:	4 cylinders. Overhead inlet valves, side exhaust valves. Bore: 100mm. Stroke: 127mm. 4084cc. 24hp. 20bhp@1000rpm. Ignition: Trembler coil
Weight:	18½cwt
Wheelbase:	9ft 1in. Track: 4ft 6in
Maximum speed:	65-70mph. Overdrive top gear
Coachbuilder:	Thos Harrington and Sons Ltd, Hove, Sussex. The body is an exact replica of the Tourist Trophy team car driven into second place by Percy Northey in the Isle of Man event in 1905

The 1905 Rolls-Royce TT replica. (Jack Sears Archive)

The 1905 30hp six-cylinder Rolls-Royce. (Jack Sears Archive)

1905 Rolls-Royce 30hp (chassis no 26355)

The car was purchased in poor condition in Australia (it had been loaded with grain). Originally, Stanley Sears owned the car in partnership with the Australian who found it, but was later able to buy out his Australian partner.

The chassis frame was bent and restoration took five years to complete. Rolls-Royce Ltd was very helpful and specially-made a new radiator, lubricator box, pump, and ignition and distributor switches. Paul Gleave and C W Morton were also extremely helpful, particularly in making a complete new Rolls-Royce carburettor to replace the original, which was missing. This necessitated drawings, patterns, castings and intricate machining.

The chassis was first fitted with a 'test rig' body for running-in and tuning. When this was completed, a new 2-seater body of 1905 type was built by Jarvis and Son of London; the car is believed to be the only surviving example of this Rolls-Royce model. It was eventually sold to Swiss collector, Tony Frey, who is the current owner.

Ownership:	First: Mrs Tate, 1 Sloane Court, London SW1; second: Sir John Barren, Sawley Hill, Ripon, Yorkshire; third: James Hunt, Victory Place, Rooney Road, London
Modifications:	New body, self-starter (non-standard)
Engine:	6 cylinders. Bore: 100mm. Stroke: 127mm. 6126cc. Valves: Overhead inlet and side exhaust. 30bhp@1000rpm
Registration no:	XAP1
Wheelbase:	9ft 4½in. Track: 4ft 8½in
Tyres:	880x120
Maximum speed:	50-55mph
Coachbuilde:	Open 2-seater by Jarvis of London

Stanley Sears and his Collection

1912 Rolls-Royce 40/50hp (chassis no 1721)

The original owner of this car was Lord Wavertree, who used it until his death. It was then stored in a barn on a farm near Wheatley, Oxfordshire, where it remained for approximately 15 years. It was covered in dust and chaff, and was extensively fouled by the droppings of poultry roosting on it and in it. In 1945 the car was purchased by S E Sears who restored it to as-new condition, including a complete overhaul of engine and chassis.

Engine:..... .... .6 cylinders, side valves. Bore: 114mm. Stroke: 121mm. 7428cc. 48.6hp. 48bhp@1200rpm
Wheelbase:. .... .11ft 11½in. Track: 4ft 8½in
Weight: 2tons 1cwt
Maximum speed:. .... .60mph
Coachbuilder:. .... .Limousine by Hooper and Co

Elegant and stylish, the 1912 Rolls-Royce 40-50 Silver Ghost limousine by Hooper. (Jack Sears Archive)

Gentleman Jack

Stanley Sears' 1914 TT Sunbeam. (Jack Sears Archive)

The engine of the TT Sunbeam. (Jack Sears Archive)

1914 Tourist Trophy Sunbeam

One of the original team cars for the Tourist Trophy in the 1914 Isle of Man event, driven by Dario Resta. It was later converted to a two-seater coupé and used for many years. It was restored by C R Abbot in 1950 to original condition with TT body. Purchased by S E Sears in 1952.

Engine:................................4 cylinders, four valves per cylinder, driven by twin overhead camshafts. 85bhp@3200rpm. Bore: 80mm. Stroke: 150mm. 3215cc. 15.9hp
Wheelbase:........................9ft 4½in. Track: 4ft 10in front; 4ft 8¼in rear
Weight:...............................22cwt
Maximum speed:..............90mph
Coachbuilder:....................Replica of original racing body built by C R Abbott

1914 Grand Prix Opel

One of the original team cars driven by Carl Joerns to 10th place in the 1914 French Grand Prix of Lyons. It was brought to England in July that year to race at Brooklands, but, owing to the outbreak of war in August, was stored in an aeroplane hangar at the track for the duration. In 1919, Henry Seagrave got it into running order and used it with success as his first racing car.

Later, it was fitted with a touring body, and, in 1948 after many years of disuse was acquired by Brian Morgan of Birmingham and completely rebuilt. Unfortunately, the cylinders were bored out too large and, on the first road trial, a burst-through to the water jackets occurred, thereby completely wrecking the block, breaking it off from the crankcase.

The car was acquired by S E Sears in 1951, who had patterns made and a new block cast. This block developed cracks in the narrow bridge between the twin exhaust valves in nos 1 and 4 cylinders. In spite of welding, repeated failure occurred until the block was distorted and useless. Two more castings were made (with smaller diameter exhaust ports) but both these showed blow holes during machining. Finally, a fourth was successful.

../..

The Stanley Sears 1914 Grand Prix Opel. (Jack Sears Archive)

GENTLEMAN JACK

Cockpit of the 1914 Grand Prix Opel. (Jack Sears Archive)

Engine:............................4 cylinders, four overhead valves per cyclinder, driven by one overhead camshaft, two magnetos. Bore: 94mm. Stroke: 160mm. 4490cc. 24hp
Wheelbase:......................9ft 2½in. Track: 4ft 6½in front; 4ft 7¼in rear
Coachbuilder:..................Replica of original racing body built by Brian Morgan in skeleton form, panelled and finished by Thos Harrington and Co Ltd of Hove, Sussex

Stanley Sears and his Collection

1914 Rolls-Royce 40/50 Alpine Eagle (chassis no 17RB)

This car was sold to Captain Millburn by James Radley in 1914, and is a sister car to the one on which Radley won the Austrian Alpine Trial during that year. Captain Milburn used it until 1932 when he presented it to Rolls-Royce Ltd, after covering over 250,000 miles. It was stored at the company's London Repair Depot until the war, when, in 1941, the body was removed and a truck body fitted. It was then used for the transport of Rolls-Royce aero engines and parts by Park Ward Ltd. After the war the body (which had been damaged) was refitted in 1947, and the car acquired by a customer who overhauled the chassis and renovated the body. He used it for a short time and then stored it in a damp garage where it deteriorated considerably. In 1951 it was purchased by S E Sears and renovated as required.

Engine:.... .... .6 cylinders, side valves. Bore: 114mm. Stroke 121mm. 7428cc. 48.6hp. 6bhp@1200rpm
Wheelbase:. .... .11ft 11½in. Track: 4ft 8½in
Maximum speed:. .... .70mph
Coachbuilder:. .... .Open 4-seater by Portholme Coach Works, London. (Owned by James Radley)

Probably the most sporting Rolls-Royce; the 1914 40-50 Alpine Eagle with Park Ward coachwork. (Jack Sears Archive)

135

1923 Rolls-Royce 20hp six-cylinder with Landaulette coachwork by Hamshaw of Leicester. (Jack Sears Archive)

1923 Rolls-Royce 20hp (chassis no 58-S1)

The original owner of this car was the Earl of Lonsdale – K G – a great friend of the Prince of Wales (later King George V). Lonsdale was also famous for his boxing trophies, the Lonsdale belts, which are still presented to British champions. Lord Lonsdale favoured yellow and black and had everything painted in this scheme.

The car was used by Lord Lonsdale until his death in 1944. The body was specially built for him in 1910 and fitted to a Daimler chassis. If it was a nice, sunny day the canvas roof of the passenger compartment could be lowered, or raised if he was in the company of a lady.

In 1923, the Earl wanted to change his car and, having tried out one of the new lower bodies that were fashionable at that time, he found that there was not sufficient headroom to accommodate the top hat he always wore. He therefore decided to retain the old body and have it mounted to the new, 20hp Rolls-Royce chassis. The car took Lord Lonsdale to every racecourse in the country. It was purchased and refurbished in 1944 by S E Sears in its familiar yellow and black. The car was sold in 1970.

Engine: 6 cylinders, overhead valves. Bore: 76mm. Stroke: 114.3mm. 3200cc. 21.6hp
Wheelbase: 10ft 9in. Track: 4ft 6in
Maximum speed: 65mph
Coachbuilder: Laundaulette by Hamshaw of Leicester, built in 1910

1927 ROLLS-ROYCE PHANTOM 1 (CHASSIS NO 76 TC)

This Phantom 1 was specially built for Mr C W Gasque of Hampstead, London, as a present to his wife. Being a connoisseur of Louis XIV style furniture, Gasque commissioned the coachbuilder to construct a miniature salon of this period inside the hansom Brougham body. The back seat was designed as a sofa; the small auxiliary seats concealed in the special bow front cabinet, which also held sherry and brandy decanters, containers for biscuits and cigarettes, and a small silver tray and glasses. The upholstery was carried out in 'petit point' needlework, commissioned at Aubusson in France. It required nine months to make and cost over £600. A French artist was brought over specially to paint the ceiling and door panels, etc. The curtains were of drawn threadwork, and the companions on each side of the seat contained fittings of genuine Battersea enamel. All external bright parts were silver-plated, and the interior metal fittings gilded. The car was used until 1937, then was laid up until 1952 when it was purchased by S E Sears, who renovated it as necessary.

Engine: .6 cylinders, overhead valves. Bore: 4½in. Stroke: 5½in. 7668cc. 43.3hp
Wheelbase: .12ft 6in, Track: 4ft 11½in
Maximum speed: .70-75mph
Coachbuilder: .Brougham by Clark of Wolverhampton

The 1927 Rolls-Royce Phantom I. (Jack Sears Archive)

GENTLEMAN JACK

The lavish 'petit point' needlework on the interior of the 1927 Rolls-Royce Phantom I by Clark of Wolverhampton. (Jack Sears Archive)

STANLEY SEARS AND HIS COLLECTION

1929 Supercharged 4½ litre Bentley

The original number 2 car of the Henry Birkin/Dorothy Paget team of road racing cars.

After passing through several owners it was purchased in 1933 by Mr Mavrogordato, who used it until the war when it was laid up in an open-fronted shed, where it deteriorated very badly owing to exposure to damp. In September 1955, it was purchased by S E Sears and completely rebuilt by Tony Townsend of Ramsbury, near Marlborough, with over 3000 hours spent in the process. In May 1959, it was taken to a closed road at Herrentals, near Antwerp in Belgium, where S E Sears covered a flying mile in both directions at an average speed of 125.676mph, thus proving that the rebuild had restored its original performance.

Today, this famous car is owned by the Volkswagen company – owner of the Bentley name – and is a star attraction in its museum.

Racing history:
1929: Irish Grand Prix. 8th at 71.9mph
1929: Tourist Trophy, Isle of Man. Crashed. (Bernard Rubin.)

../..

Jack Sears sets off in the Brighton Speed Trials with the Tim Birkin 4.5 litre supercharged Bentley. (Jack Sears Archive)

Probably one of the best known racing Bentleys, the 1929 Supercharged 4.5 litre, commonly known as the Tim Birkin car, used by Birkin and Jean Chassagne to win the Brooklands Double Twelve Hour race in 1930. (Jack Sears Archive)

Gentleman Jack

The impressive cockpit of the Birkin Bentley. (Jack Sears Archive)

1930: Double Twelve Hour Race. Driven by Sir Henry Birkin and Jean Chassagne
1930: Le Mans 24 Hour Race. Driven by Sir Henry Birkin and Jean Chassagne. Lap record by Birkin at 89.69mph
1930: Irish Grand Prix. 4th at 78.85mph. Driven by Sir Henry Birkin
1930: Tourist Trophy, Isle of Man. Class lap record at 76.2mph. Driven by Sir Henry Birkin
1930: BR.DC 500 mile race at Brooklands. 2nd at 112.12mph. Driven by Dr J D Benjafield and E R Hall

Engine:.... .... .4 cylinders. Bore: 100mm. Stroke: 140mm. 4398cc. 24.8hp. Four valves per cylinder operated by a single overhead camshaft. Two magnetos. Villiers supercharger giving a maximum pressure of 10lbs/sqin
Wheelbase:.. .... .10ft (special short chassis). Track: 4ft 10in
Weight: ... . .2 tons
Maximum speed:. .... .126mph
Coachbuilder:. .... .Van den Plas

1931 Bentley 8 litre

Over the years this car was extensively and continually developed by L C McKenzie to give reduced weight and more speed. The original chassis side frame members were removed, and new side frame members from a Bentley 4 litre chassis substituted to reduce the wheelbase from 12 to 11 feet. The entire car was lowered by cutting down the radiator and lowering the springs. Weight was reduced as much as possible throughout, including fitting a new duralumin body.

The engine was progressively tuned – via improvements to the exhaust and inlet systems, including fitting 3 carburettors and special high compression pistons etc – to give a final maximum bhp of approximately 340.

On the death of Mr Forrest Lycett in April 1960, the car was acquired by S E Sears in accordance with mutual arrangements previously made.

Records:
In Mr Forrest Lycett's hands the car held several Class records including:
   Shelsey Walsh Hill Climb
   Lewes Speed Trials
   Brighton Speed Trials
   Brooklands Track 29th August 1939, Class B. British standing start mile record 92.9mph (This was the last record ever taken before the track was closed)

Belgium, Jabbeke July 1950, Class B Belgian national records:
   Flying Km 16.60 seconds/134.755mph
   Flying Mile 26.90 seconds/133.828mph

../..

The famous 1931 Forrest Lycett 8 litre Bentley that set a number of speed records on the Belgian Jabbeke road in 1950. In 1939, this car set a British Standing Start mile record of 92.9mph, the last record at Brooklands before the track was closed. (Jack Sears Archive)

The impressive six-cylinder, 8 litre Bentley engine in the Forrest Lycett car. (Jack Sears Archive)

    Standing Km 27.21 seconds/82.210mph
    Standing Mile 38.54 seconds/93.405mph
(These records stood until 1958)

Belgium, near Antwerp May 1959, Class B Belgian national records:
    Flying Km 15.35 seconds/141.131mph
    Flying Mile 26.90 seconds/140.845mph
    Standing Km 27.04 seconds/82.726mph
    Standing Mile 37.76 seconds/95.338mph

Engine: .6 cylinders. Bore: 110mm. Stroke: 140mm. 7983cc. 44.0hp. Four valves per cylinder operated by overhead camshaft
Wheelbase: Originally 12ft but shortened to 11ft Track: 4ft 8 in
Length: 14ft 10 in
Width: 5ft. 8in
Weight: Originally 2½ tons, now 33cwt
Tyres: Originally 2½ tons x 21in, now 7inx19in rear, 6.00x19in front
Coachbuilder: Originally open 4-seater by Corsica; now fitted with specially light duralumin-framed racing 2-seater

1932 Rolls-Royce 20/25hp (chassis GZU 30)

The first owner of this 20/25 was Walter Dunster of Sanderstead, Surrey, who used the car until August 1948 when it was sold to Charles Goode-Parker of Guildford. It remained in his ownership until November 1953 when it was purchased by S E Sears. The engine was rebored at 53,750 miles.

Engine:..... .... .6 cylinders, overhead valve. Bore 82.5mm. Stroke: 114mm. 3669cc. 25.3hp
Maximum speed:. .... .75mph
Weight: ... . .1 ton 17¼ cwt
Wheelbase:. .... .11ft. Track: 4ft 8in
Coachbuilder:. .... .Sports saloon by Thrupp and Maberley

1932 Rolls-Royce 20/25 sports saloon by Thrupp and Maberley.
(Jack Sears Archive)

Rolls-Royce Phantom II (1932) Sedanca de Ville by Barker:
six-cylinder, 7.6 litre. (Jack Sears Archive)

1934 ROLLS-ROYCE PHANTOM II (CHASSIS NO 3 RY)
This Phantom II was originally owned by J Abrahams & Sons Ltd, and used as the managing director's personal car until it was purchased by S E Sears in March 1955. Re-cellulosed in 1956.

Engine:.... .... .6 cylinders, overhead valves. Bore: 4¼in. Stroke: 5½in. 7668cc. 43.3hp
Wheelbase:. .... .12ft 6in. Track: 4ft 10½in front, 5ft rear
Maximum speed:. 80-85mph
Coachbuilder:. .... .Sedanca de Ville by Barker

1938 ROLLS-ROYCE PHANTOM III (CHASSIS NO 3-DL-76)

Stanley Sears took his mother to the Olympia Motor Show in 1938 and persuaded her that she should have a new car. The car chosen was a beautiful maroon, close-coupled Rolls-Royce Phantom III Limousine by Thrupp and Maberley. A year later war started and, what with petrol rationing and the fear of German bombers in Sussex, Stanley drove the Rolls-Royce to his mother's house on the Helford river in Cornwall, and left it there for the duration of hostilities.

Engine: 12 cylinders in 60 degree V, overhead valves. Bore: 3¼in. Stroke 4½in. 7340cc. 50.7hp
Maximum speed: 90-95mph
Wheelbase: 11ft 10in. Track: 5ft 0.6in front, 5ft 2.6in rear
Coachbuilder: Close-coupled limousine by Thrupp and Maberley

1938 V12 Rolls-Royce Phantom III purchased new at the London Motor Show in October 1938 for Mrs Caroline Sears, Jack's grandmother. (Jack Sears Archive)

GENTLEMAN JACK

The newest Rolls-Royce in the Stanley Sears collection was this 1939 Wraith, with two-door sports body by James Young of Bromley. (Jack Sears Archive)

1939 ROLLS-ROYCE WRAITH (CHASSIS NO WEC 2)

This car was first registered in April 1941 by Mr W Harvey of Bradford on Avon. In January 1950, it was sold to Mr L Wynn-Owen of Bishops Waltham, and used by him until January 1959 when it was purchased by S E Sears. The car was then overhauled as necessary and the engine rebored.

Engine:.... .... .6 cylinders, overhead valves. Bore: 3½in. Stroke: 4¼in. 4257cc. 30hp
Wheelbase:. .... .11ft 4in. Track:4ft 10½in front, 4ft 1½in rear
Maximum speed:. .... .80mph
Coachbuilder:. .... .2-door sports saloon by James Young and Co Ltd of Bromley

146

The three Rolls-Royce Phantom models owned by Stanley Sears.
Left to right: the Phantom III, Phantom II and Phantom I.
(Jack Sears Archive)

APPENDIX 2
RACE & RALLY STATISTICS

The following table details Jack Sears' racing and rallying performances from the year 1950, when he first began to keep meticulous records of his career. Information about events before 1950 are contained within the book's text.

Date	Event	Car	Notes	Result
1950				
	BARC Eastbourne Rally	MG TC		5th overall, 2nd in Class 1st Class award
	Veteran Car Club Radley Rally	Clement Talbot	This 1903 car was owned by Stanley Sears	3rd in Class
	Veteran Car Club Eastbourne Rally	Rolls-Royce	The 1912 Rolls owned by Stanley Sears	3rd in Class
	BARC Goodwood Members Meeting	MG TC	Five lap race for 1500cc sports cars	6th overall
1951				
May	Vintage Sports Car Club, Silverstone	Sunbeam TT	This 1914 car was run in an Edwardian handicap event	2nd overall
July	Brighton and Hove Motor Club Rally	MG TCS	By now the MGTC had been fitted with a Wade supercharger	4th overall, 2nd in Class
Aug	20 Ghost Club Driving Tests	Rolls-Royce Alpine	A 1914 car, registration no 17RB	1st in Class
Aug	Veteran Car Club Dorking Hill Climb	Sunbeam TT		3rd in formula, 1st in Class
Sept	Vintage Sports Car Club Prescott Hill Climb	Sunbeam TT		1st in Edwardian Class
Nov	MCC *Daily Express* National Rally	MG TCS		3rd in Class
1952				
Mar 22	Vintage Sports Car Club Pomeroy Trophy, Silverstone	Sunbeam TT		6th overall
Mar 31	RAC International Rally of GB	Vauxhall Velox	Owned by Jack's mother and loaned to him for the rally	16th in Class
Apr 1	Bristol Motor and Light Car Club, Castle Coombe	Cooper-MG	6 lap scratch race The car ran in the 1100-1500cc Class	2nd in Class
Apr 19	London Motor Club Little Rally	Jaguar XK120	Won the team prize with Walter Grant-Norton and Carl Richardson	1st Team

Race & Rally statistics

Date	Event	Car	Notes	Result
Apr 26	VCC Hendon Rally Driving Tests	Sunbeam TT		2nd in Class IV
May 3	VSCC, Silverstone	Sunbeam TT	Finished 3rd in the Itala Trophy and 6th in the 10 lap handicap	3rd & 10th
May 17	BARC Goodwood Members Meeting	Cooper-MG	Two races; 5th in the scratch race and 3rd in the handicap event	5th & 3rd
May 24	Maidstone & Mid Kent MC, Silverstone	Cooper-MG	Scratch race for 1100-1500cc sports cars	4th
June	Cheltenham MC Staverton Speed Trials	Cooper-MG		2nd in Class
Jul 12	VSCC, Silverstone	Sunbeam TT	Handicap event for Edwardians	3rd
Jul	VCC Dorking Hill Climb	Sunbeam TT		FTD
Aug 16	VSCC, Prescott	Sunbeam TT	Second fastest Edwardian	3rd
Sept	Brighton & Hove MC driving tests	Cooper-MG		1st overall

1954

Date	Event	Car	Notes	Result
Mar 6	Cirencester CC '500 Mile Rally'	Jaguar XK120	Reg DVV 200. Member of winning team	2nd in Class
Mar 9	RAC International Rally	Jaguar XK120		3rd in Class 31st overall
Mar 26	VSCC Pomeroy Trophy, Silverstone	Sunbeam TT	Jack's first Pomeroy Trophy win	1st overall 1st Edwardian
Apr 4	West Essex CC Wethersfield Sprint	Jaguar XK120	One kilometre sprint course, time 31.40sec	2nd in Class
Apr 19	Half Litre CC, Brands Hatch	Lister-MG	1500cc sports car race. Fastest in practice	2nd overall
Apr 24	Aston Martin OC, Snetterton	Lister-MG	Fastest lap 2min .04sec (78.4mph). Sports cars up to 2000cc	6th overall
Apr 25	International Tulip Rally	Alvis 3 litre	Co-driver with J W E Banks	6th overall, 2nd in Class
May 1	VSCC, Silverstone	Sunbeam TT	Itala Trophy run on handicap. 5th on scratch but 1st in handicap. Special award for fastest race average	1st overall
May 8	West Hants and Dorset CC, Ibsley	Lister-MG	Fastest in 1500cc race in practice: 1:35.8. Retired on start line due to ignition problems	
May 9	Bugatti OC, Prescott	Lister-MG	Time: 50.7	3rd in Class
May 29	Eight Clubs, Silverstone	Lister-MG	5th in scratch race and 4th in handicap	5th & 4th
May	London MC Sprint, Goodwood	Jaguar XK120	Using Woodcote corner and the chicane	4th unlimited, 6th in general
June 5	West Essex CC, Snetterton	Lister-MG	Set up fastest lap 2:06 1500cc scratch Handicap race 2nd	1st & 2nd
June 6	Snetterton MRC, Snetterton	Jaguar XK120 Lister-MG	1st over 2 litres with the Jaguar, 2nd in 1500cc race with Lister	1st & 2nd
Aug 2	Half Litre Club, Brands Hatch	Sunbeam TT	2nd Edwardian Handicap and fastest lap	
Aug 14	West Essex CC International, Snetterton	Lister-MG	Jack finished 3rd in the 1500cc Class behind Kenneth McAlpine (Connaught) and John Coombs (Lotus-Connaught) Also fastest lap	3rd
Sept 5	Bentley Drivers Club, Firle Hill Climb	Jaguar XK120		3rd in Class
Oct 2	Snetterton MRC, Snetterton	Jaguar XK120	Fastest lap	2nd in Class
Oct 9	Eastern Counties MC, Snetterton	Jaguar Xk120		2nd Class, 3rd handicap
Oct 16	Snetterton	Morris Oxford	A 24 hour endurance test of a Morris Oxford. Other two drivers were Oliver Sear and David Allen	Average 54.67mph
Oct 23	Sporting CC of Norfolk Ten Test rally	Jaguar XK120 Coupé		1st in Class, 8th general

1955

Date	Event	Car	Notes	Result
Mar 8	RAC Rally of GB	Renault 750	Renault UK-entered car; co-driver Tony Hind	2nd Class 1

GENTLEMAN JACK

Date	Event	Car	Notes	Result
Mar 26	Snetterton	Lister-Bristol	First race with 4 CNO. Raced in 1500-2700cc Class	2nd in Class
April 2	British Empire Trophy, Oulton Park	Lister-Bristol	Heat 2: finished 5th in 1501-2700. Final: finished 19th (see text)	5th and 19th
Apr 11	Goodwood International	Lister-Bristol	Retired in 2 litre race with puncture when lying 3rd. Fastest in practice	
Apr 16	VSCC Silverstone	Opel GP	Driving 1914 Opel Grand Prix car in the Edwardian race. Retired with slipping clutch. Itala Trophy: retired with broken universal joint. Lapped 5 seconds faster than with the TT Sunbeam	
May 7	International Silverstone	Lister Bristol	Crashed during sports car race. Overturned at Copse Corner due to engine cutting out and drifting into the bank	
May 30	International Goodwood	Sunbeam TT		2nd
Jul 6	VCC Silver Jubilee rally	1905 Rolls-Royce	Winner of the Regent Trophy Aksi 1st in concours and tests	1st overall
Jul 30	International Crystal Palace	Lister-Bristol	Timing chain broke in practice	
Aug 1	International Brands Hatch	Sunbeam TT	Edwardian Handicap	1st
Aug 13	International Snetterton	Lister Bristol	Retired last lap in 2 litre race with wire off ignition switch	
Aug 21	VSCC Prescott HC	Sunbeam TT	Edwardian Handicap. Over 3000cc Class	2nd & 2nd
Sep 4	Brands Hatch	Lister-Bristol		3rd
Sep 11	Eastern Counties Speed Trial	Lister Bristol	2000cc Class. 2000cc Class Esses Trophy	1st & 1st
Sept 17	BRSCC/BRDC National Silverstone	Lister–Bristol	2000 cc Class	1st
Sept 25	Snetterton	Lister-Bristol	Unlimited sports cars. 2000cc sports handicap	5th & 1st
Oct 1	International Castle Coombe	Lister-Bristol	Two Litre Trophy Race. Invitation sports car race	2nd & 1st
Oct 9	Brands Hatch	Lister-Bristol	Over 1900cc sports	2nd
1956				
Jan 15	Monte Carlo Rally	Austin A50	With Archie Scott Brown and Ken Best. Crashed but classified	6th in Class, 76th overall
Mar 6	RAC Rally of GB	Austin A50	With Peter Garnier	3rd in Class 6, 1st in team
April	Eastern Counties MC, Snetterton Speed Trial	FCB	Standard 10 special with a wooden body owned by Sir Bill Bunbury	1st Class award
May 6	International Tulip Rally	Austin A90	With Syd Henson and Richard Bensted-Smith	2nd in Class
May 19	West Essex CC, Snetterton	FCB		2nd
May 25	Geneva Rally	Austin A50	With Ken Best	1st in Class
June 3	Thames Estuary Sprint, Snetterton	FCB		1st in Class
July 6	Alpine Rally	MGA Hardtop	With Ken Best. Crashed on last day 150 miles from finish when 5th overall	
Sept 17	Viking Rally	Austin A105	With Ken Best	5th in Class
Nov 4	London-Brighton Run	1904 Mercedes	With Ken Best. Finshers' plaque	
1957				
Feb 26	Sestriere Rally	Austin A105	With Ken Best	6th in Class
Mar 10	Cambridge University MC driving tests	Austin A105	Overall. Saloon Class	3rd & 2nd
May 6	Tulip Rally	Austin A105		41st overall, 4th in Class
May 19	Snetterton MRC, Snetterton	Austin A105		1st saloon
June 15	VSCC Silverstone	Sunbeam TT	Edwardian Handicap	5th

Race & Rally Statistics

Date	Event	Car	Notes	Result
July 27	BRSCC Silverstone	Austin A105	Second to John Webb with a Jensen 541	
Aug 5	BRSCC National, Brands Hastch	Austin A105	Heinkel Trophy for saloons	1st
Sept 1	SMRC, Snetterton	Austin A105		1st
Sept 14	BRDC Daily Express Trophy, Silverstone	Austin A105	2000-3000cc Class. Winner Harold Grace, Riley, 2nd Ron Flockhart 2.4 Jaguar (Coombs)	3rd
Oct 6	BRSCC, Brands Hatch	Austin A 105	Saloon car race	1st
Oct 26	Snetterton 24 hour run with Borgward	Borgward Isabella	With Tom Bridger, Brian Fry, Tony Hind and Mike McKee	62.0mph
Oct 27	SMRC Speed Trial, Snetterton	Austin A105	Over 1500cc saloons	2nd
1958				
Jan 12	Monte Carlo Rally	Austin A105	With Sam Moore and Ken Best. Disqualified because over 1 hour lateness in terrible snow	
Mar 12	RAC Rally of GB	Austin-Healey 100/6	With Peter Garnier. Six port head and disc brakes	52nd overall, 6th in Class
Mar 30	SMRC Snetterton	Austin A 105	Saloons 2000-3000cc	1st
April 7	BRSCC Brands Hatch	Austin A 105	John Davy Trophy saloons	1st in Class
April 12	VSCC, Silverstone	Sunbeam TT Maserati GP	Edwardian Handicap. First single seater drive in Nobby Spero's ex-Seaman Maserati	2nd & 2nd
April 20	BRSCC, Brands Hatch	Austin A105	1600-2700cc saloons	1st
April 26	Tulip Rally	Austin-Healey 100/6	With Peter Garnier. Retired with broken distributor drive when 2nd in Class and 10th overall	
May 3	BRDC Daily Express, Silverstone	Austin A105	2000-3000 saloon Class	2nd
May 11	BRSCC, Mallory Park	Austin A105	Fastest lap	2nd
May 18	BRSCC, Brands Hatch	Austin A105	1600-2700cc Class	1st
May 26	BARC, Goodwood	Austin-Healey 100/6	Marque race	1st
June 9	BRSCC, Brands Hatch	Austin A105	1601-2700cc	1st
June 29	ECMC !00 mile saloon race, Snetterton	Austin A105	Won team prize with John Sprinzel (A35) and Tom Sopwith (Jaguar 3,4)	
July 6	Alpine Rally	Austin-H ealey 100/6	With Sam Moore. Overall 11th 1600cc GT Class	5th
July 19	British GP, Silverstone	Austin A105	Class 2001-3000cc	1st
Aug 5	BRSCC Brands Hatch	Austin A105 Sunbeam TT	Now with 3 carburettors. Edwardian Handicap	1st in Class & 2nd
Aug 30	International, Brands Hatch	Austin A105	Winner of Class	1st
Sept 6	Brighton Speed Trials	Austin-Healey 100/6	Marque Class	3rd
Sept 7	SMRC Snetterton	Austin-Healey 100/6	GT car race	1st
Oct 5	BRSCC, Brands Hatch	Austin A105	Class winner. Now equal with Tommy Sopwith in British Saloon Championship. Won the run off	1st
Oct 11	SMRC, Snetterton	Austin-Healey 100/6	One hour GT race	2nd
Oct 26	SMRC Sprint, Snetterton	Austin-Healey 100/6	1601-3000cc Class	4th

Total season earnings: £837-5/-

1959				
Mar 22	SMRC, Snetterton	Austin-Healey 100/6	GT race fastest lap	2nd
Mar 30	BRSCC, Brands Hatch	Austin-Healey 100/6	GT race	1st
April 11	VSCC, Silverstone	Sunbeam TT	Edwardian Handicap	1st
April 19	BRSCC, Snetterton	Austin-Healey 100/6	GT Race	1st

GENTLEMAN JACK

Date	Event	Car	Notes	Result
April 27	Tulip Rally	Austin-Healey 100/6	With Peter Garnier PMO203. General classification 8th. Also FTD at Zandvoort and Interland Team Trophy with Keith Ballisat and Cuth Harrison	1st GT
May 2	International Trophy, Silverstone	Austin-Healey 100/6	GT race. Behind Stirling Moss and Roy Salvadori	3rd
May 9	Maidstone & Mid Kent MC, Silverstone	Austin-Healey 100/6	GT race	2nd
May 10	SMRC Snetterton	Austin-Healey 100/6	Pushed off the track by Peter Woozley	
May 18	Nottingham SCC, Mallory Park	Austin-Healey 100/6	GT race	2nd
June 14	ECMC, Snetterton	Jaguar 3.4 Austin-Healey	Entered by Tommy Sopwith. Led until brakes failed. GT race	2nd & 4th
June 23	Alpine Rally	Austin-Healey 3000	With Sam Moore. Retired on Vivione Pass fan through radiator problem	
July 12	BRSCC, Brands Hatch	Austin-Healey 3000	Marque race	1st
July 26	Vanwall Trophy, Snetterton	Austin-Healey 3000	Over 2000cc Autosport Round. GT race over 2000cc	3rd & 3rd
Aug 3	BRSCC Brands Hatch	Austin-Healey 3000	Over 2000cc Autosport Round	3rd
Aug 9	National Benzole Trophy, Snetterton	Austin-Healey 3000	Over 2000cc Autosport Round. Won by Dick Protheroe in Jaguar XK120	2nd
Aug 29	Internatinal Meeting, Brands Hatch	Jaguar 3.4	Equipe Endeavour car. Saloon car race	1st
Sept 2	Liège-Rome-Liège Rally	Austin-Healey 3000	With Peter Garnier. Fog and navigational error caused retirement	
Sept 13	NSCC, Mallory Park	Austin-Healey 3000	Autosport qualifier	2nd
Sept 26	Gold Cup, Oulton Park	Austin-Healey 3000	Over 2000cc Autosport	1st
Oct 10	Three Hour Race, Snetterton	Austin-Healey 3000	Final of Autosport Championship. Over 2000cc Class	2nd
Nov 21	RAC Rally of GB	Austin-Healey 3000	With Willy Cave SMO746. 17th in general classification. GT Class	2nd
1960				
Mar 26	Sebring 12 hour race	Austin-Healey 3000	With Peter Riley. In UJB 143 2500-3000 Class	3rd
April 18	International Goodwood	Jaguar 3.8	Saloon car race. Sopwith car. Third behind Stirling Moss, Roy Salvadori	3rd
April 30	BARC International, Aintree	Aston Martin DB4GT	Equipe Endeavour car. Gt race	1st
May 7	National Race, Oulton Park	Aston Martin DB4GT	Closed car race	1st
May 14	International Trophy, Silverstone	Aston Martin DB4GT	International Sports Car Race. Car completely outclassed	13th
May 22	National Meeting, Snetterton	Aston Martin DB4GT	Closed Car Race	1st
June 6	National Meeting, Crystal Palace	Cooper-Climax	Formula 2 race driving the Yeoman Credit Cooper. Equal fastest lap	3rd
June 19	National Race Meeting. Snetterton	Jaguar 3.8	Touring car race. Equipe Endeavour	1st
June 23	Le Mans 24 hrs	Austin-Healey 3000	With Peter Riley UJB143. Retired when lying 8th with big ends gone due to oil seal	
July 16	British GP, Silverstone	Jaguar 3.8	Touring Car Race. Shared fastest lap with Colin Chapman (Jaguar), who won	2nd
August 1	International Race, Brands Hatch	Aston Martin DB4GT. Jaguar 3.8	GT race. Touring Car Race	1st & 2nd
August 6	SMRC Vanwall Trophy, Snetterton	Cooper-Climax	Vanwall Trophy. Yeoman Credit car, retired due to ignition problems	
August 27	International Race, Brands Hatch	Jaguar 3.8 Aston Martin DB4GT	Touring Car Race. Farningham Trophy. GT race Redex Trophy, second to Stirling Moss in Ferrari 250GT	1st & 2nd
Nov 21	RAC Rally of GB	Jaguar 3.8	With Willy Cave. Peter Berry Jaguar. Won *Motor Sport* Trophy	4th overall, 1st in Class

Race & Rally Statistics

Date	Event	Car	Notes	Result
1961				
Mar 25	Lombank Trophy, Snetterton	Jaguar 3.8	Lying 2nd to Michael Parkes; both ran out of fuel. Coasted to line	5th
Apr 15	National Meeting, Oulton Park	Ferrari 250 Berlinetta	Equipe Endeavour car. GT race	4th
Apr 22	International 200, Aintree	Jaguar 3.8	Touring car race won by Salvadori. Third and fourth were Bruce McLaren and Michael Parkes	2nd
May 22	National Meeting, Crystal Palace	Jaguar E-type / Jaguar 3.8	GT race. Touring Car race; eased off the track by Roy Salvadori, bent back axle	2nd
July 15th	British Grand Prix, Silverstone	Jaguar E-type	John Coombs car, beaten by Lex Davison in Aston Martin Zagato due to overheating	2nd
July 23	Archie Scott Brown Memorial, Snetterton	Jaguar 3.8	Equipe Endeavour car VCD400	1st
Aug 7	International, Brands Hatch	Jaguar 3.8	Beaten by Parkes and Salvadori due to failing brakes	3rd
Sept 2	Brighton Speed Trials	Bentley 4.5 Supercharged	Time 34.9 seconds	
Sept 3	Bentley DC, Firle Hill Climb	Bentley 4.5 Supercharged	33.01sec. Father, Stanley Sears, recorded 32.56sec!	
Sept 30	Molyslip Trophy, Snetterton	Jaguar E-type	Finished fourth behind Parkes, Salvadori and Ireland	4th
1962				
Mar 24	12 Hour Sports Car race, Sebring	MGA Mk II	With Andrew Hedges. Finished behind two Porsches and a Sunbeam	4th
Apr 7	Trophy Meeting, Oulton Park	Jaguar 3.8	Equipe Endeavour car JAG400 behind Roy Salvadori	2nd
April 14	Lombank Trophy, Snetterton	Jaguar 3.8	Behind Michael Parkes and ahead of Graham Hill and Roy Salvadori	2nd
April 23	International Meeting, Goodwood	Jaguar 3.8	Behind Graham Hill and Roy Salvadori	3rd
April 28	International 200, Aintree	Jaguar 3.8	Behind Hill, Salvadori and David Hobbs	4th
May 10	International Trophy, Silverstone	Jaguar 3.8	Behind Hill and Parkes	3rd
June 11	Whit Monday, Crystal Palace	Jaguar 3.8	Behind Salvadori	2nd
July 15	Archie Scott Brown, Snetterton	Jaguar 3.8	Car withdrawn after Tommy Sopwith lost a wheel in other team car	
July 21	RAC British GP, Aintree	Jaguar 3.8	Ex-Berry car 687DXA. Ahead of Parkes and Sir Gawaine Baillie	1st
Aug 6	International Meeting, Brands Hatch	Jaguar 3.8	Molyslip Trophy Race. Beaten by Michael Parkes	1st
Sep 1	Gold Cup Meeting, Oulton Park	Jaguar 3.8	Equipe Endeavour car VCD400. Beaten by Graham Hill	2nd
Sept	Tour de France rally	Jaguar 3.8	With Claude Lego who owned the car. Serious crash at Clermont Ferrand	
1963				
Mar 23	Pomeroy Trophy, Silverstone	Sunbeam TT	Won Pomeroy Trophy for second time	1st
Mar 30	Lombank Trophy, Snetterton	Ford Cortina GT	Entered by John Willment but withdrawn due to homologation problem	
Apr 6	Spring Meeting, Oulton Park	Ford Cortina GT	Now homologated. First outing	4th overall, 1st in Class
Apr 15	International Goodwood	Ford Cortina GT		7th overall, 1st in Class
Apr 27	International, Aintree	Ford Cortina GT		4th overall, 1st in Class
May 11	International Trophy, Silverstone	Ford Galaxie	First appearance of the NASCAR Galaxie	1st overall

Gentleman Jack

Date	Event	Car	Notes	Result
May 25	100 Mile race, Aintree	Ford Galaxie		1st overall
June 3	International, Crystal Palace	Ford Galaxie		1st overall
June 15	Le Mans 24 Hour race	Ferrari 330LMB (4725GT)	Maranello Concessionaires	5th overall, 1st in Class
July 6	International 6-Hour, Brands Hatch	Cortina GT		3rd overall, 1st in Class
July 13	International, Mallory Park	Ferrari 250GTO (4399GT)	Maranello Concessionaires	2nd overall, 1st in Class
July 14	Scott-Brown Memorial, Snetterton	Ford Galaxie	Two races, winner of both	1st overall
July 20	British GP Meeting, Silverstone	Ferrari 250GTO (4399GT) Ford Galaxie	Maranello Concessionaires car	5th & 1st overall
Aug 5	International, Brands Hatch	Ferrari 250GTO (3729GT) Ford Galaxie	John Coombs car. Retired (puncture)	4th overall
Aug 18	Marlboro USA	Ford Cortina GT	First US race for Cortina GT	1st overall, 1st in Class
Aug 24	Tourist Trophy, Goodwood	Jaguar E-type	John Coombs	4th overall, 2nd in Class
Sept 1	International, Zandvoort	Ford Cortina GT		1st in Class
Sept 14	International, Brands Hatch	Ford Cortina GT		1st in Class
Sept 21	Gold Cup, Oulton Park	Ford Cortina Lotus	Entered by Team Lotus. First appearance of the Lotus Cortina	3rd overall, 1st in Class
Sept 28	International 3 hours, Snetterton	Ferrari 250GTO (3729GT)	John Coombs car	4th overall, 2nd in Class
Nov 02	Kyalami 9 Hours South Africa	Ford Galaxie	Blown cylinder head gasket. Co-driven by Paul Hawkins	
1964				
Mar 14	Snetterton	Ford Galaxie	Retired	
Mar 30	Goodwood	Ford Galaxie. AC Cobra	Saloon car race. Sports	1st overall & 2nd
Apr 11	Oulton Park	Ford Galaxie. AC Cobra	Saloon car race: retired. GT race	2nd
Apr 18	Aintree	Ford Galaxie. AC Cobra	Saloon car race. Sports	1st & 3rd
Apr 25	Intl Trophy Silverstone	Ford Galaxie	Saloon car race	1st
May 2	Silverstone	Ford Galaxie. AC Cobra	Saloon car race. GT race	1st & 3rd
May 10	Zolder	Ford Galaxie	Saloon car race	1st
May 16	Aintree	Ford Galaxie	Saloon car race	1st
May 18	Crystal Palace	Ford Galaxie	Saloon car race: retired with puncture	
June 6	Brands Hatch	Cortina GT	Saloon car race	4th
June 13	Crystal Palace	Ford Galaxie	Saloon car race	1st
June 20	Le Mans 24 Hours	AC Cobra Coupé	Retired in GT Class	
July 11	Brands Hatch	AC Cobra. Lotus-Cortina	GT race. Saloon car race	1st & 2nd
July 19	Snetterton	AC Cobra. Ford Galaxie	GT race: retired	1st
July 26	Cascais, Portugal	Ford Cortina	Saloon car race	1st
Aug 3	Brands Hatch	AC Cobra. Ford Galaxie	GT race. Saloon car race	1st & 1st

Race & Rally Statistics

Date	Event	Car	Notes	Result
Aug 22	Croft	AC Cobra. Ford Galaxie	GT Race. Saloon car race	1st & 1st
Aug 29	Tourist Trophy, Goodwood	AC Cobra	Second in GT Class	4th overall
Sept 19	Oulton Park	Ford Galaxie	Retired	
Sept 26	Snetterton	Cobra Coupé	Willment-built car	1st
Oct 31	Kyalami 9 hrs	AC Cobra	Sports car Class	5th

1965

Date	Event	Car	Notes	Result
Mar 13	Ilford Films Trophy, Brands Hatch	Ford Lotus-Cortina	Retired on lap 18 with a puncture	
Mar 20	Silverstone	Ford Lotus-Cortina	Meeting abandoned because of rain	
Mar 26	3 hour saloon race, Sebring	Ford Lotus-Cortina	Team Lotus entered Jim Clark and Jack for this race. Clark was winner	2nd
April 3	Oulton Park	Ford Lotus-Cortina	Saloon car race. Retired first lap; engine problems	
April 10	Snetterton	Ford Lotus-Cortina		3rd
April 19	Goodwood	Ford Lotus-Cortina. Willment Cobra	St Marys Trophy. Sussex Trophy	2nd & 2nd
April 25	Monza 1000	Shelby American Cobra	With Sir John Whitmore	11th, 2nd in Class
May 1	Tourist Trophy, Oulton Park	Shelby American Cobra		7th overall, 4th in Class
May 15	Silverstone	Ford Lotus-Cortina. Lotus 30	Senior Service Touring Car Race. 25 lap sports car race	3rd overall, 1st in Class & 3rd overall
May 23	Nürburgring 1000km	Shelby American Cobra	With Frank Gardner	10th overall, 3rd in Class
June 7	Crystal Palace	Ford Lotus-Cortina	Norbury Trophy	3rd overall, 2nd in Class
June 13	Nürburgring 6 Hour Saloon car race	Ford Lotus-Cortina	Won with Sir John Whitmore ahead of the Pierpoint/Neerpasch Mustang	1st overall
June 19	Le Mans 24 Hours	Shelby American Cobra	With Dick Thompson	8th overall, 1st in Class
July 3	Reims 12 Hours	Shelby American Cobra	With Sir John Whitmore	9th overall, 2nd in Class
July 10	Silverstone	Ford Lotus-Corina	Touring Car Race, Tied with Sir John Whitmore, Lotus Cortina	Joint 3rd. Joint 1st in Class
July 24	Martini Trophy, Silverstone	Ford Lotus-Cortina		2nd overall, 1st in Class
Aug 13	Enna 4 hour race	Shelby American Cobra		4th overall, 2nd in Class
Aug 30	Guards Trophy, Brands Hatch	Willment Cobra Coupé. Ford Lotus-Cortina	Ilford Films Trophy	1st overall, 1st in Class & 4th overall, 1st in Class
Sept 11	Brighton Speed Trials	Sunbeam TT		
Sept 12	Firle Hill Climb	Bentley 8 litre	Fastest time of the day by a Bentley	
Sept 18	Gold Cup, Oulton Park	Ford Lotus-Cortina		3rd overall, 2nd in Class

Bibliography

In addition to the people above one must also refer to a host of articles and extracts from magazines like *Autosport*, *Motor Sport*, *Motoring News* and contemporary newspaper stories. Charles Harbord for extracts from a series of his articles in *Cars for the Connoisseur*.
Also information from the following books:

Archie and the Listers (Robert Edwards)
Cooper Cars (Doug Nye)
Daytona Cobra Coupés (Peter Brock, Dave Friedman, George Stauffer)
Ferrari 250GTO (Keith Bluemel with Jess G Pourret)
Powered by Jaguar (Doug Nye)
Roy Salvadori – Racing Driver (Anthony Pritchard)
Triumph and Tragedy (Yves Kaltenbach)

MOTOR RACING
Reflections of a lost era
Anthony Carter

ISBN: 9781904788102 £39.99

BRM
A MECHANIC'S TALE
DICK SALMON
In collaboration with ANTHONY CARTER

Foreword by BETTE HILL

ISBN 9781845840822 £39.99

p&p extra; call 01305 260068 for details or visit www.veloce.co.uk (prices subject to change)

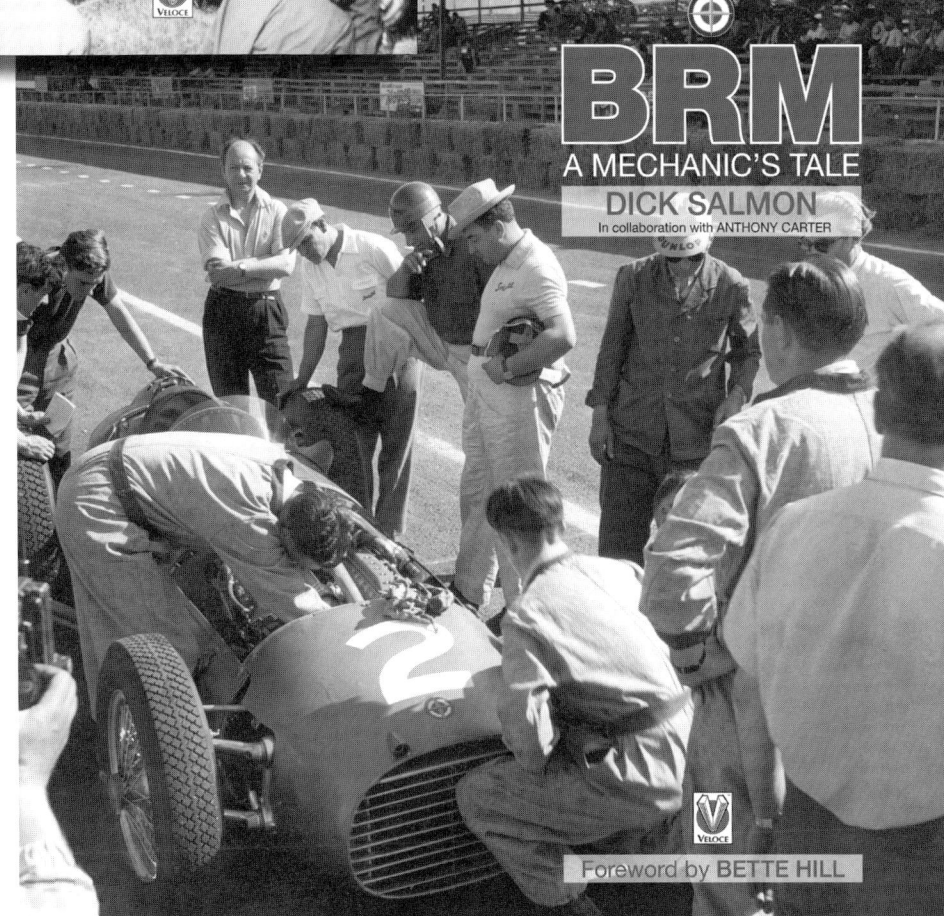

RALLYE SPORT FORDS
The inside story
Mike Moreton

ISBN: 9781845841157 £24.99

From the Fells to Ferrari
The Official Biography of Cliff Allison
Graham Gauld : Foreword by Dan Gurney

ISBN: 9781845841508 £22.50

– Revised Paperback Edition –
THE MGA
John Price-Williams

ISBN: 9781903706565 £24.99

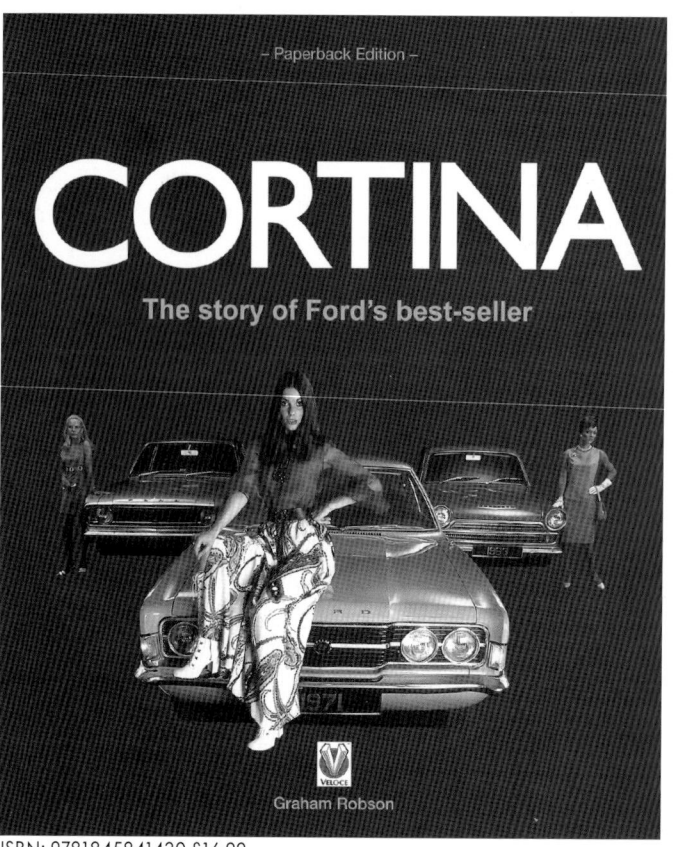

– Paperback Edition –
CORTINA
The story of Ford's best-seller
Graham Robson

ISBN: 9781845841430 £16.99

p&p extra; call 01305 260068 for details or visit www.veloce.co.uk (prices subject to change)

INDEX

AC Cobra Coupé 74
Aitken, Sir Max 100, 103
Allen, Cullimore 10
Allen John and Sons 10
Alpine Rally 34
Alvis 22, 23
Ambrose, Tony 103, 104
Arundel, Peter 72
Ashburn Shield 13
Aston Martin DB4GT 40-42, 44
Atco Junior 9, 12
Austin A50 31
Austin A 105 36-38
Austin-Healey 33, 39, 40, 44, 46-48

Baillie, Sir Gawaine 36, 59, 60, 65, 123
Bandini, Lorenzo 70
Banks, Bill 22
Banks, Warwick 22
BARC 15
Barricello, Rubens 117
Bassett-Lowke 20
Bedwell, Hey 14, 15, 22
Berry, Peter 52, 56
Best, Ken 30
Black, Bill 24
Blakes of Liverpool 17, 27
Blumer, Jimmy 71
Bolney Grange 10
Bolton, Peter 75-77
Bondurant, Bob 87, 88, 90
Bourdais, Sebastien 117, 120
BMC 23, 31, 36
BRDC 23, 99, 103
Bridger, Tommy 32
Brighton & Hove MC 15
Brighton Speed Trials 13, 15
BRP 49
British Saloon Champ 36, 39, 73
Bugatti 10
Bunbury, Sir William 15, 31, 82
Byrne, Rory 114

Castle Coombe 17
Cave, Willie 40, 52
Chambers, Marcus 32, 33, 36, 40, 44, 46
Chapman, Colin 50, 51, 73, 84, 86, 93, 115
Charterhouse 13, 15, 113
Cirencester 15, 17

Clark, Jim 32, 73, 83, 84, 93
Clement-Talbot 9, 121
Clermont Ferrand 59, 60
Clore, Charles 19
Cobra Daytona Coupé 82, 88
Colgate, John 45
Collingtree Grange 7, 9, 19, 20, 121
Consten, Bernard 59, 60
Coombs, John 40, 50, 51, 55, 70
Cooper F2 49
Cooper-MG 17, 19, 20
Cooper-Jaguar 46
Corner, Neil 107
Cowan, Andrew 105
Crombac, Jabby 92
Crystal Palace 49

Darracq 9, 121
Dickens, Arthur 8
Dixon, Nick 113

Eason-Gibson, John 68
Elliot, Frank 26
Enever, Sydney 33
Endeavour Equipe 36, 39, 44, 55, 60
England, Lofty 50, 59

FCB 31
Ferrari 250GT 42, 48, 52
Ferrari, Enzo 61
Ferrari GTO 69-71, 80, 107
Ferrari 330LMB 67, 69-71
Ferrari Owners Club 61, 108
Firestone 64
Firman, Ralph 115
FN 13
Ford Cortina GT 64, 71
Ford Galaxie 64-68
Ford Lotus Cortina 72-74, 87
Ford Zephyr 36, 44
Forrest Lycett 123, 141, 142
Foster, Cal 115
Freeman Hardy Willis 19

Ganassi, Chip 116
Garnier, Peter 39
Goodwood 15, 30
Gott, John 34
Gregory, Ken 49, 50
Gurney, Dan 64, 67, 75, 87

Hampton, Peter 10
Harbord, Charles 69
Hawthorn, Mike 38, 43
Hayes, Walter 85
Hedges, Andrew 55
Hill, Graham 36, 40, 55, 64, 70, 73
Hind, Tony 23, 32
Hoare, Col Ronnie 42, 52, 61, 67, 69-71
Hollman & Moody 64, 72
Hounslow, Alec 33
HRG 1500 15
Hulbert, George 36
Hurlock, Derek 76

Inoue, Taki 115

Jaguar Drivers Club 32
Jaguar XK120 17, 20, 21
Jaguar 3.4 36, 40, 43
Jaguar 3.8 41, 52, 53, 63
Jaguar E-Type 53
Jane, Bob 55-58

Kirkpatrick, John 112

Lawton, George 50
Lego, Claude 58, 59
Le Mans 46-48, 67, 69, 117
Liège-Rome-Liège 39
Lister, Brian 22, 24
Lister-Bristol 24-27
Lister-MG 20, 22
London Motor Club 19
Lotus 30/40 96, 97

Mann, Alan 72, 85, 87, 88, 91
Mansell, Nigel 113
Marang, Andre 59
Marlboro Circuit 71
Marquart, Jo 117
Maserati 32, 33
McKee, Kenneth 31, 32, 60, 99
McKee, Mike 31, 32, 50, 99
McQueen, Steve 55
Mercedes 1904 11
MGA MkII 54
MG TC 13, 14
Monte Carlo Rally 27, 31
Montoya, Juan Pablo 117, 119
Monza 33
Morgan 13
Morley Twins 39, 40, 52
Mors 122
Morton Cavendish 15
Moss, Alfred 49
Moss, Pat 33
Moss, Stirling 49, 54

Olthoff, Bob 70-72, 85
Oulton Park 24, 43

Packer, Frank/Kerry 101, 104
Panther Mr 8
Parkes, Michael 55-57, 61
Parnell, Reg 26
Pilette, Teddy 117
Piper, David 80
Pledger, Bill 46
Prescott Hill Climb 17

RAC Rally 19, 23, 52
Reece, Peter/Jackie 17, 27
Renault 750 23, 24
Resta, Dario 16

Riches, Fred 15
Riley 1.5 36
Riley, Peter 15, 39, 44, 45.
Robinson, Tony 49
Rolls-Royce 1905 30, 122
Royale 113
Russell, Jim (School) 50, 111

Salmon, Michael 69
Salvadori, Roy 40, 50, 54, 58, 64
Scott-Brown, Archie 20, 24, 27, 31, 110
Schneider Trophy 42
Sear, Oliver 15, 31
Sears, Caroline 7, 19
Sears, Cicely 20, 30, 48, 64, 85, 86, 107
Sears, David 10, 30, 50, 106, 110-120
Sears, Diana 32, 107, 108
Sears, Eric 9, 13
Sears, Florence 8
Sears, Jennifer 10, 85, 98
Sears, Jack 9, 12, 20
Sears, John and Co 8, 9, 19
Sears, John Snr 7, 8
Sears, Lilian 9
Sears, Stanley Edward 8-10, 15
Sears, Suzanne 10, 50, 85, 109, 110
Sears Holdings 15
Sebring 44, 45, 46, 54, 86
Sebring Sprite 54
Shelby, Caroll 75, 88, 90
Silverstone 16
Simmons, David 15
Snetterton 15, 24, 50
Snetterton MRC 15, 31
Sopwith Sphinx 43
Sopwith, Tommy 36, 38-40, 43, 49, 54, 60, 100
Sopwith, Sir Thomas 42
Speedwell Engineering 36, 39
Spero, Nobby 32, 33, 50
Sprinzel, John 36
SS Chusan 105
Staub, Georges 13
Stevens, Jocelyn 100
Stewart, Jackie 78, 80, 81
Sunbeam, TT 16, 17, 21
Sunley, Bernard 19
Super Nova 117

Taylor, Henry 28, 49, 71, 82, 83
Taylor, Trevor 32, 49
True-Form, 17, 19
Tulip Rally 23, 39
Turner, Stuart 82
Tye, Basil 80

Uphall Grange 15, 19, 20, 100, 110
Uren, Jeff 36, 62, 70, 79

Vauxhall 9, 11
Vauxhall Velox 19
Veteran Car Club 10, 121
VSCC 17

Walkinshaw, Tom 115
Whitmore, Sir John 70, 82, 86, 88
Willment Cobra 82, 85
Willment Racing Team 64, 82
Wood, Barry 26

Yeoman-Credit 49
Yoong, Alex 117

159

Autodrome
The lost race circuits of Europe
S.S. Collins & Gavin D. Ireland

ISBN: 9781904788317 £35.99

1½-litre Grand Prix Racing 1961-65
– Low Power, High Tech
Mark Whitelock

ISBN: 9781845840167 £39.99

p&p extra; call 01305 260068 for details or visit www.veloce.co.uk (prices subject to change)